FERMENTING
RECIPES & PREPARATION

Daphne Lambert has cooked, studied, taught and written about food all her adult life. She was the co-owner and chef of a multi-award winning organic restaurant. Daphne has regularly contributed recipes and articles to numerous books and magazines and is the author of three books on food and health. She has run a nutritional consultancy practice for 25 years looking at ways to nourish wellbeing and is the founding member of Greencuisine Trust, an educational charity, where she brings to her work as a nutritionist and educator her passion for food that truly nourishes body, mind and soul.

Publisher & Creative Director: Nick Wells
Senior Project Editor: Catherine Taylor
Copy Editor: Kathy Steer
Art Director: Mike Spender
Layout Design: Jane Ashley
Digital Design & Production: Chris Herbert
Proofreader: Dawn Laker

Special thanks to Jenna Cordisco

FLAME TREE PUBLISHING
6 Melbray Mews, Fulham,
London SW6 3NS, United Kingdom
www.flametreepublishing.com

This edition published 2016

Picture Credits

Alamy Stock Photo/MIXA 140. © StockFood and the following: 7l Blake, Anthony; 9tr Crossland, Don; 66l Maximilian Stock Ltd; 71tr Gräfe & Unzer Verlag / Fotos mit Geschmack; 71b Kerth, Ulrich; 78 & 79 Eising Studio - Food Photo & Video; 123 Foodcollection; 124 Wissing, Michael; 127 Vråskar, Veslemøy; 129 , 191 Gräfe & Unzer Verlag / Lang, Coco; 130 Bischof, Harry; 145, 195 Gräfe & Unzer Verlag / Riis, René; 157 Gräfe & Unzer Verlag / mona binner PHOTOGRAPHIE; 166 Foodfolio; 175 Gräfe & Unzer Verlag / Rynio, Jörn ; 179 Janssen, Valerie; 181 Alack, Chris; 193 Stowell, Sam; 196 Blend Images; 204 Caste, Alain; 211 India Picture; 221 PhotoCuisine / Bilic, Jérômes. Courtesy Shutterstock.com and the following: 1 & 76 Ivan Volozhanin; 3 & 83 sebra; 4 Wollertz; 6l, 22t, 212–13 Arina P Habich; 6r Foodio; 7r Olena Kaminetska; 9tl Gossip; 9b Hummy; 13t MosayMay; 13bl Pergame; 13br, 68bl stockcreations; 14l, 57br Natalia Klenova; 14r Zju4ka; 15l espies; 15r Raihana Asral; 16–17 Taesik Park; 18 Anton_Ivanov; 19 Romaset; 21tl Elena Larina; 21bl Jiri Hera; 21br momente; 21tr Pirtuss; 22br Ekaterina Kondratova; 22bl NatashaPhoto; 25 Rawpixel.com; 27 aleksandr hunta; 28r Olivier Le Queinec; 28l Ursula Ferrara; 29l miunicaneurona; 29r, 37r Monkey Business Images; 30–31 Lumena; 32r lassedesignen; 32l pajtica; 33l Christian-Fischer; 33r Foodpictures; 34 & 138–139 nada54; 36l merc67; 36r, 72t vm2002; 37l Kittibowornphatnon; 39 ch_ch; 40–41, 133 Ehpoint; 43bl, 84l casanisa; 43t joannawnuk; 43br tacar; 44r, 121 AS Food studio; 44l, 111 DUSAN ZIDAR; 45r, 77 Africa Studio; 45l Letterberry; 46–47 ChiccoDodiFC; 49tl, 58 iravgustin; 49tr Oksana Shufrych; 49b successo images; 50r kazoka; 50l ziashusha; 51l KenKitti; 52 viennetta; 54l Ievgeniia Maslovska; 54r Tatiana Vorona; 55r 135pixels; 55l Nishihama; 57bl, 115 blackboard1965; 57t sasimoto; 61tr Andreas Kraus; 61tl ballphotographer; 61b Suto Norbert Zsolt; 62–63, 97 marekuliasz; 65, 75 Anna Hoychuk; 66r Pavlo Burdyak; 67l Crepesoles; 67r Viorel Sima; 68t Karpenkov Denis; 68br R_Szatkowski; 71tl melima; 72br Igor Zubkis; 72bl, 151 Tanya Stolyarevskaya; 80–81 rebvt; 84r Devin_Pavel; 85l Creative Photo Corner; 85r haraldmuc; 87 mythja; 91 Stock image; 93 Magdalena Paluchowska; 99 SiberianLena; 104–105 Auhustsinovich; 107 Lilyana Vynogradova; 108 Shulevskyy Volodymyr; 113 Ganihina Daria; 116 Wiktory; 135 Elena Elisseeva; 137 Jerry-Rainey; 147 HandmadePictures; 148 picturepartners; 155 Melica; 158 Magdanatka; 161 Joshua Resnick; 162–163 verca; 165, 219 Brent Hofacker; 171 5PH; 172 Apelavi; 182–183 Vinogradov Illya; 185 PG Studija; 187 Natalia Evstigneeva; 201 Yulia Davidovich; 203 Sea Wave; 207 JOAT; 209 Jyothi Rajesh; 215 Paul_Brighton; 217 Liesel Fuchs.

FERMENTING
RECIPES & PREPARATION

Daphne Lambert

FLAME TREE
PUBLISHING

CONTENTS

INTRODUCTION

With the industrialization of food and farming, many traditional artisan fermented foods disappeared from our Western diet, but recently there has been a renewed interest in these foods, including fermented food from around the world.

BUYING & MAKING FERMENTED FOOD

Some of our favourite foods obtain their complexity of flavour from the process of fermentation – tangy cheese and sourdough breads, fiery kimchis, sour pickles and tart yogurt are all fermented foods – and our ever-growing interest means there are plenty to choose from in the markets and shops.

However, there is immense pleasure in making your own. Mostly it is surprisingly simple and despite a complex biochemical process at work in each ferment, all you have to do is create the right environment and the microorganisms will do the rest.

EVERY FERMENTING CREATION IS UNIQUE

Whatever you create will be unique to you and your kitchen because the ferments will be affected by the many different varieties and strains of microorganisms that live in your environment. From the San Francisco sourdough rye to the lait ribot from Brittany and from Japanese miso to cultured butter from Devon, the taste, aroma and flavour comes from each unique environment.

Handcrafted products like artisan ferments contain the spirit of the land on which they were grown together with the spirit of the person whose hands created the delicious food.

If you are beginning your fermentation journey, start simply with a few lacto-fermented vegetables, along with some beverages like kefir or kvass, and slowly build up your repertoire. Ferments are always alive and changing, so enjoy the taste of each one, as it's hard to repeat the exact same flavour each time!

ABOUT THIS BOOK

If you are a more seasoned fermenter this book offers lots of opportunities to further explore your relationship with microbes and make a variety of nourishing dishes.

The first section shares a little history and introduces you to the key fermented foods, tools and equipment that are helpful, plus a few principles and techniques. The second part, after a few basic recipes, offers a selection of dishes that demonstrate the endless possibilities with fermented foods. Some of the ferments in the recipe section do not give exact quantities, as they are more about method, so the amount each recipe makes is determined by you the fermenter!

THE HEALTH BENEFITS

Many fermented foods have tremendous health benefits – nutrients are more bioavailable, foods easier to digest and lacto-fermented foods, in particular, are full of beneficial bacteria. It's important to eat a range of ferments raw to take advantage of the probiotic bacteria, but occasionally, you can enliven cooked dishes with their vibrant flavours. Add them at the end to minimize the chances of the probiotic bacteria being destroyed by the heat.

Love your ever-growing relationship with microorganisms and above all enjoy the delicious flavours of your ferments.

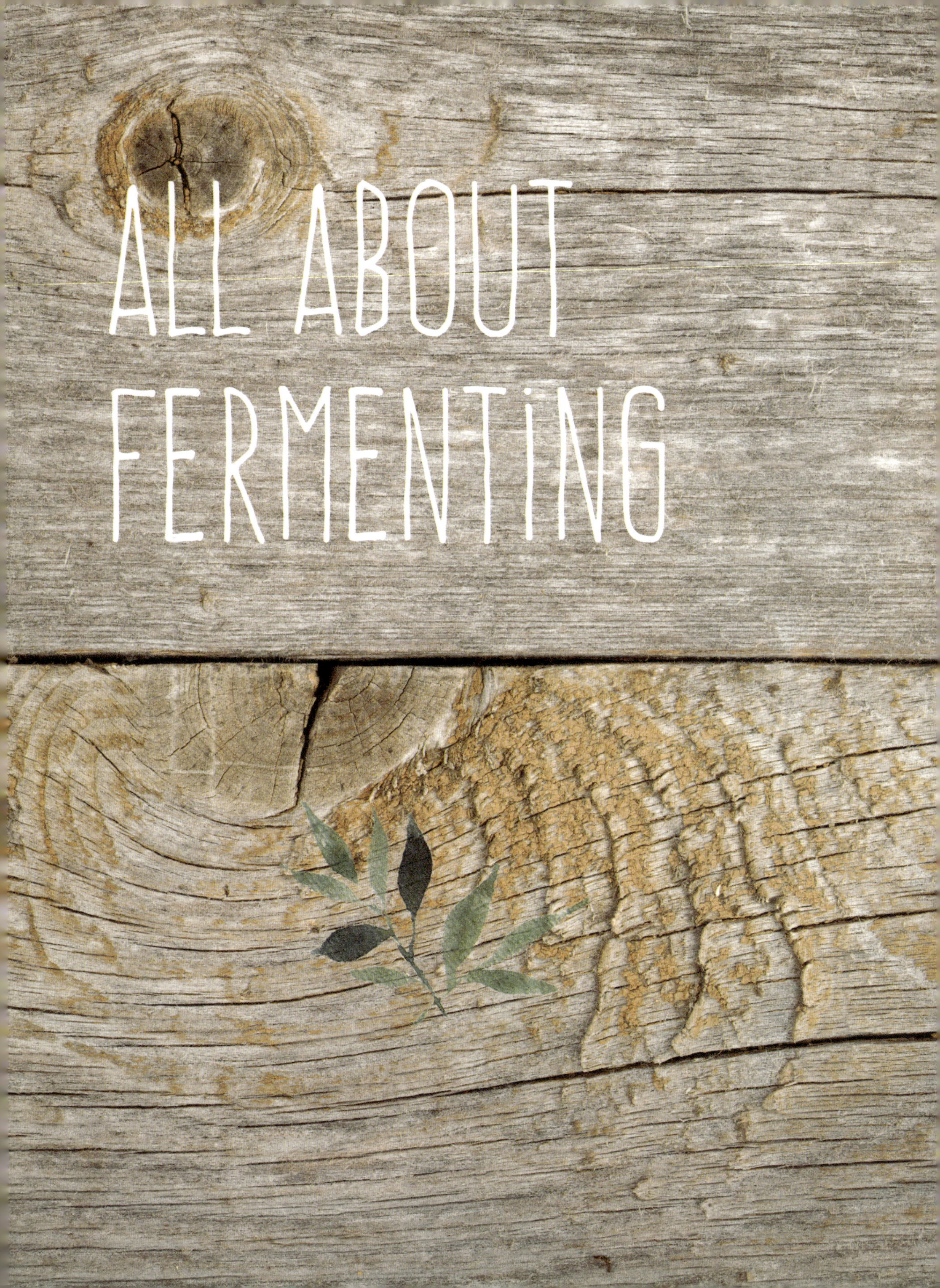

ALL ABOUT
FERMENTING

A HISTORY OF FERMENTING

The history of fermentation stretches back into the long distant past, and no one can be certain how we learnt to adapt this natural phenomenon to become such an integral part of so many food cultures. From the dawn of civilisation the fermentation process has preserved food and brought us a wealth of flavours, textures and innumerable health benefits.

WHAT IS IT?

More than three billion years ago bacteria ignited life on planet earth through the process of fermentation, so this process has been with us since the beginning of time! Fermentation occurs when microorganisms find food to eat, and in the process of nourishing themselves, create biochemical changes in the organic material from which they are deriving their energy and significantly change its nature.

How We Have Used Fermentation

Humans have learnt to work with this process, harnessing the power of beneficial microorganisms namely bacteria, yeasts and moulds to transform food. During the process different 'bio preservatives' – lactic acid, acetic acid or ethyl alcohol – are created. Careful control of this natural process can result in a preserved food that is both delicious and nutritious.

Although the process of fermenting foods and beverages has been used for thousands of years, for most of that time it must have been seen as a mysterious and magical transformation. Understanding the microbial and enzymatic processes that are responsible for the transformation is relatively recent.

WHEN DOES IT DATE BACK TO?

Fermented drinks, including meads, wines and beers have been around for thousands of years. One of the earliest pieces of evidence of an alcoholic beverage comes from residues of a fermented drink made of grapes, hawthorn berries, honey and rice, which were discovered on 9,000 year-old pottery shards in the Neolithic settlement of Jiahu in China. Evidence suggests that alcohol has had a significant influence since these times be it one of forbiddance, or more often worship. They seem to have been integral in honouring the dead, as examples of ancient alcohol-related funeral rituals have been discovered throughout the world.

Who Used Fermented Food?

Writings and drawings from around the world show that nearly every civilisation since early times has included fermented food in their culture. Many of the fermented milk products we are familiar with today were developed by nomadic Asian cattle breeders.

Fermented breads can be traced back to the Egyptians about 3,500 years ago and fermented meat sausages to the Babylonians around 1500 BC.

After drying, fermentation is the oldest method of preservation and most foods such as legumes, vegetables, grains, meat, fish and dairy have a long history of being cultured with microorganisms. The varieties of fermented foods and drinks that evolved depended on the raw materials that were available in a local environment together with cultural taste preferences.

CULTURAL DIVERSITY

The unique flavours of Korean kimchi, Indian idli, West African gari, Native American Cherokee bread, Alaskan stink-head, Egyptian laban, Vietnamese mám and Indonesian tempeh, many of which are essential components of everyday cuisine, demonstrate the importance of fermentation in defining the world's diverse food traditions.

Traditional food cultures used fermentation to make food as nutritious as possible, and knowledge and skill about various ferments would have been passed down from generation to generation; for example, sharing information on how to ferment grains to increase the bioavailability of nutrients or how to ferment cassava to remove harmful toxins, which enabled nourishing foods to be made. One of the main advantages of fermentation for our ancestors was the conversion of perishable foods into storable products, which provided food for less productive seasons.

WHY WAS FERMENTATION USED?

Fundamentally fermentation was used throughout the world as a survival strategy. In regions of harsh temperatures a high proportion of foods eaten would have been fermented. In cold climates, it was impossible to grow and unrealistic to try to catch food in the winter, so during the summer months when the ice melted, fish and birds were caught, buried in pits and left to ferment until the winter when food was scarce.

In hot tropical countries fermentation made sure food was transformed into something nutritious, rather than allowing the tropical heat to decompose the food and make it inedible. It is well documented how important fermented foods were to the traditional Alaskan diet. Stink-head, made from salmon heads, and muktuk, a delicacy of fermented seal flipper, were essential foods to the Alaskans when the days were short and cold and there was little winter produce to be found.

The Indigenous Fermented Foods of the Sudan Hamid Dirar suggests 90 fermented foods made by the Sudanese. Here in one of the hottest and driest countries in the world a range of raw ingredients were fermented, from cereals and milk to bones and locusts.

SCIENTIFIC UNDERSTANDING

Our modern understanding of fermentation comes from the work of French chemist Louis Pasteur, who in 1854 determined that the fermentation process was caused by

yeast. This discovery was followed by the work of German chemist Eduard Buechner, who showed it was the enzymes in yeast cells that caused fermentation. Pasteur, who initially researched the fermentation process in making wine, went on to discover that there were two types of fermentation: alcoholic fermentation caused by the action of yeast and lactic acid fermentation caused by the action of bacteria.

HOW IS IT USED?

Since the time of Pasteur the growing scientific understanding of the process of fermentation has enabled us to manipulate and control fermenting processes so well that large-scale production of fermented foods has evolved, especially milk products like yogurt and cheese; meat products like salami, prosciutto di Parma, beef bresaola and sausages, along with an enormous variety of beers and wine. In recent years fermentation processes have also been used in other industries including producing energy from biomass, making drugs like antibiotics and the production of industrial enzymes for use in the food and detergent industries.

TRANSFORMATIVE ENZYMES

The transformation of food through fermentation is the result of enzymes produced by the microorganisms bacteria, yeasts and moulds. Enzymes are protein catalysts that break down complex organic molecules to form smaller compounds, which are able to pass through the cell walls of microorganisms enabling them to grow and thrive. The by-product of this process can be a nourishing food for us.

THE DIFFERENT TYPES OF FERMENTATION

There are three types of fermentation: lactic acid, ethyl alcohol and acetic acid.

Even cocoa beans are fermented in the chocolate-making process

Lactic acid fermentation occurs when yeasts and bacteria convert starches and sugar into lactic acid. Ethyl alcohol fermentation is the conversion, by beneficial microorganisms, of carbohydrates into alcohol; and acetic fermentation takes place when alcohol is exposed to air.

Bacteria

Bacteria are the largest group of microorganisms. Many people have been led to believe they are harmful, but the truth is very few of them are pathogenic and many of them are extremely beneficial.

Lactobacillaceae are the most important family of bacteria used in food ferments. Bacteria are partially, or wholly, responsible for many of our much-loved foods, including yogurt, coffee, cheese and chocolate. A second group of bacteria are the acetic acid producers, which are used in the production of vinegar.

Yeasts

Yeasts are microscopic single-celled fungi living mostly on sugars and starches from which they produce carbon dioxide gas and alcohol. Yeasts generally of the Saccharomyces genus are responsible for the rising of bread dough and fermenting alcoholic beverages.

Moulds

Moulds are multicellular fungi that grow well in moist, warm conditions. Moulds from the genus Penicillium are associated with the ripening of cheese, and tempeh is made by inoculating cooked soybeans with the genus Rhizopus. In general, most food fermentations are not the result of a single culture but different species of bacteria, various yeasts and moulds all taking part together.

DECLINE & RENAISSANCE

While many cultures, especially in India, Africa and Japan, have always had fermented foods as an integral part of their food cultures, in the West, during the twentieth century they slowly became less important. The decline was primarily due to the arrival of refrigeration along with the centralisation of food production and the growth of 'convenience' foods. In recent years, however, we have seen a renaissance of interest in fermented foods, due mainly to our growing knowledge and understanding of how beneficial these foods can be to our health, and we want to know where our food comes from and how it is produced. We have begun to make nourishing foods in our homes again and communities are sharing kitchens and beginning to make fermented foods together, often from produce grown on nearby allotments or shared gardens.

THE MOST BENEFICIAL FERMENTED FOODS

Although we have become increasingly aware of the health benefits associated with eating fermented foods, we should be aware that not all fermented foods have the same health-giving properties. The most beneficial ones are those that contain probiotic and prebiotic bacteria, as in lactic-fermented vegetables. Luckily, these are the easiest ones to start making at home!

WHY FERMENT?

There are a host of good reasons for including fermented food and beverages in your diet. For many people, the main reason for wanting to include them is simply the health benefits associated with these foods. Links between fermented foods and health together with their use as medicine can be traced back as far as Ancient Rome and China.

FERMENTED FOOD AS MEDICINE

Consumption of fermented milks containing live bacterial cultures have long been associated with good health. As far back as 76 BC, the Roman historian Plinio recommended raw fermented milk products, believing they could treat intestinal disorders.

The thirteenth-century Mongolian warrior Genghis Khan is said to have encouraged his army to drink a fermented horse milk yogurt called kumis. He believed kumis would keep them healthy as well as make them brave. A similar horse milk yogurt in Russia, called koumiss, has long been regarded as a highly nutritious food and considered therapeutic. Today it is still part of the treatment offered in Russian sanatoria particularly for pulmonary tuberculosis.

Preventing Disease

In 1768 when Captain Cook set sail to the South Pacific, he took on board over 7,000 pounds of sauerkraut to prevent scurvy. During the seventeenth and eighteenth centuries, many a seafarer died as a result of this dreadful disease, which is caused by a lack of vitamin C. It was important to find a solution and it was hoped the humble cabbage, fermented to last the long journey, would provide the answer. Indeed it did, as fermented cabbage is a particularly good source of vitamin C and when a daily ration was given to the sailors, scurvy was prevented.

Making koumiss

The medicinal use of the Japanese fermented umeboshi plum can be traced back over 1,000 years. Umeboshi are still used today in Japan as a 'cure-all' medicine for a whole range of disorders as well as a general tonic.

Russian scientist Elie Metchnikoff suggested in 1907 that regularly drinking sour milk, rich in 'Bulgarian bacillus', accounted for the health and longevity of Bulgarian peasants. He hypothesized that replacing putrefactive bacteria in the gut with lactic acid bacteria would enhance health, and scientific research went on to prove him right!

WHAT ARE THE HEALTH BENEFITS OF FERMENTED FOODS?

The fermentation process pre-digests food, which in turn makes it easier for you to digest. During this process nutrients become more bioavailable, extra nutrients are formed and toxins are removed. Fermented foods that are rich in lactic-acid forming bacteria are especially good for you as they help to support a healthy gut.

Above left: Umeboshi plums are a typical fermented fruit

What Do We Mean By 'A Healthy Gut'?

Trillions of microorganisms live in our gut, including over 400 species of bacteria. These microorganisms, collectively known as our gut microbiota – or th emicrobiome – weigh in about 2 kg/4½ lb. For our gut to be healthy, the majority of these microorganisms must be ones that are beneficial to us. These beneficial bacteria perform a mind-boggling array of tasks, including synthesizing the B group of vitamins as well as vitamin K, promoting the absorption of minerals, ensuring proper digestion and helping to develop and regulate the immune system. Evidence suggests that the composition of the bacteria in our gut affects obesity, diabetes, eczema and rheumatoid arthritis.

The gut microbiota also play an important role in healthy brain development. In particular, microbiota seem to influence the development of the brain regions involved in our response to stress, along with anxiety, depression and a range of different behavioural patterns.

A well-balanced microbiome, full of beneficial bacteria, keeps harmful microorganisms in check by neutralizing toxins, inhibiting yeast growth and crowding out the pathogenic bacteria. The composition of these microbiota can become disrupted by a number of factors – stress; environmental chemicals, including pesticides and insecticides; antibiotics; lifestyle and your choice of food.

Keeping a Balance

Our modern-day Western diet has processed out many naturally occurring beneficial bacteria, and at the same time, increased the foods on which any pathogenic bacteria residing in our gut just love to feast, namely refined carbohydrates and especially sugar. A balanced microbiome that is healthy, strong and protective needs the right nourishment from the foods you eat. Foods that contain prebiotics and probiotics exert a beneficial effect on the gut microbial balance and they are two of the most widely studied elements that play a part in keeping a balance.

What Are Prebiotics?

Prebiotics provide food for and stimulate the growth of the beneficial bacteria in the gut. Prebiotics are classified as a soluble fibre, and inulin and oligofructose are the two most important ones for providing nourishment to gut bacteria. Also referred to as fermentable fibre, prebiotics are naturally present in a range of vegetables and fruit especially garlic, onions, leeks, asparagus, Jerusalem artichokes, plums and bananas.

What Are Probiotics?

Probiotics are live bacteria that can bring about health benefits when eaten. These beneficial live bacteria colonize the gut, helping to maintain a healthy microbiome. Probiotics, however, must survive in the acidic gastric environment if they are to reach the small intestine, colonize the host and impart their benefits. The best-known and researched are Lactobacillus and Bifidobacterium, which are particularly good at surviving the acid environment in the stomach.

Prebiotics are fermentable fibre, including leeks, onions and garlic

Other microorganisms including Enterococcus and Streptococcus have also been studied. Many probiotics come from bacteria traditionally used for fermenting food. Two of the best sources of probiotics are lacto-fermented vegetables and lacto-fermented milks.

Many fermented foods, especially lacto-fermented vegetables, provide a good source of both prebiotics and probiotics, making them a potent food for supporting gut health. Prebiotics are not destroyed by heat; probiotics, on the other hand, are, so to ensure the full benefits of probiotics, lacto-fermented foods and beverages are best consumed raw.

WHAT ARE THE OTHER BENEFITS OF FERMENTED FOODS?

Beyond the process of breaking down food, which makes it far easier to digest, and helping to restore the proper balance of bacteria in the gut with beneficial prebiotics and probiotics, there are also a number of other benefits associated with fermented foods.

Fermentation Preserves Foods

Fermentation preserves foods thus extending shelf life and is also a good way of not wasting a surplus. In addition it is a convenient way of storing food. For many people, especially in developing countries, preserving food through fermenting gives them greater food security.

Creates More Nutrients

Fermenting organisms increase certain vitamins, especially B vitamins, including thiamin, riboflavin and niacin. The fermentation process breaks down proteins into simple amino acids, fats into fatty acids and carbohydrates into simple sugars and in the process creates greater bioavailability of nutrients. Fermented foods also often contain a higher level of convertible energy than non-fermented foods of the same weight.

Degrades 'Anti-nutrients' & Removes Toxins

In various grains and legumes fermentation effectively breaks down phytate (or phytic acid) and lectins. Phytate is a bioactive compound widely distributed in plant foods that can bind to minerals in your gut and prevent their absorption into your body, which can lead to mineral deficiencies (especially if you do not consume the right balance of nutrients to counteract these effects or your body has particular trouble digesting such foods). Many lectins are inflammatory, as they can disrupt the lining of the gut wall, leading to a condition known as leaky gut syndrome. Soybeans are particularly high in both phytate and lectins. Fermentation also deactivates enzyme inhibitors, enabling protein to be better digested. Cassava is a staple food in many parts of Africa and Asia and with some varieties fermentation is absolutely essential as the process removes the toxic compound cyanide, so making it edible.

Raw Fermented Foods Are a Good Source of Enzymes

Your body needs enzymes to properly digest and metabolize your food. Over time, the body loses its ability to manufacture enzymes (which are mostly produced by the pancreas and liver). Young adults have 30 times the enzymes of the elderly. When we constantly eat food that is deficient in enzymes our bodies are forced to make the necessary enzymes to digest our food, and this can then lead to compromises in making other enzymes that are needed in the body for repair and renewal.

The research of Dr Edward Howell, a pioneer in the field of food enzymes, concluded that if you ate an enzyme-rich diet you could live a longer, healthier life. Eating raw fermented foods, on which the action of bacteria has produced enzymes, is a good way of contributing enzymes to your diet.

Fermentation is Energy Efficient

The energy resources used by our food takes into account the energy embedded in the food's growth and transport as well as the energy used in cooking and refrigeration. Fermented foods are particularly energy efficient as they reduce the need for both cooking and refrigeration.

Inexpensive

Fermenting vegetables, grains and dairy is easy and inexpensive. Generally you need to buy minimal equipment and mostly you can improvise.

It's Fun & It Tastes Good!

Fermenting is a really great way of connecting – with bacteria, food and friends. It is a good sharing activity that brings people together around the kitchen table, to chop and pound, laugh and taste delicious ferments. It's immense fun and the end result of bubbling crocks, bottles and jars of tasty food and drink will enliven your meals and health.

KEY FERMENTED FOODS

There is a whole range of fermented foods that you can either make or buy. Many fermented foods have been available to buy for a long time, but others have only recently appeared in shops and markets.

DAIRY-BASED

Nearly every culture has developed some kind of fermented dairy product. In the West, cow's milk is the most popular milk used for dairy products, followed by goat, ewe and buffalo. Around the world other mammals are milked, including horses, camels, llamas and reindeer.

Yogurt

Yogurt is one of the best-known fermented dairy products and is produced using two active lactic cultures of bacteria, Lactobacillus bulgaricus and Streptococcus thermophilus. It is easy to source these cultures to start making your own yogurt at home or you can start the process with a little bought live culture yogurt with no added sugars or stabilizers.

Kefir

Milk kefir is made from white gelatinous clumps that resemble cauliflower florets and are called grains. These grains ferment the milk, creating a cultured product full of beneficial bacteria. According to legend the grains were a gift from Allah delivered to his people by Muhammed. The kefir preparation was to be kept secret, otherwise the grains would lose their magic power. Fortunately the sharing of the grains has not led to the demise of their power and the refreshing drink can be enjoyed by everyone. Kefir is readily available to buy, but also easy to make yourself (*see* page 108).

Top: Milk kefir grains; Bottom left: Kefir; Bottom right: Yogurt

Cheese

Cheese is made from milk by fermenting with special bacteria. There are endless varieties of cheese, with each variation determined by the pasture, milk, environment and particular microorganisms. There are two main families of lactic acid bacteria, Lactococci and Lactobacilli, that are important in the initial ripening of cheese. In addition, certain moulds play an important role. Two species of blue mould, Penicillium roqueforti and Penicillium glaucom, give rise to the myriad blue cheeses that can be found globally. White moulds are found on a variety of soft, ripened cheeses and are generally a subspecies of Penicillium camembertii.

When you buy cheese, try to source artisan varieties made preferably from unpasteurized milk (if they're pasteurized, any potentially friendly gut bacteria will have been killed off). If you want to make your own cheese, start with the relatively simple acid curd cheeses like fromage frais and cottage cheese.

Crème Fraîche

Crème fraîche is made by culturing cream with a little lactic acid bacteria and leaving it at room temperature to thicken and acquire a slight tang. This kind of cream is far more stable to cook with and will last in the refrigerator for up to three weeks. Readily available to buy, you can also make crème fraîche yourself by stirring buttermilk into cream.

Cultured Butter

Before pasteurisation and refrigeration, raw cream naturally soured, quite quickly, overnight through the action of lactic bacteria. The butter that was made from churning this cream had deep, rich overtones. Today most butter available to buy is not cultured, but it is making a comeback and can be bought in specialist shops and online. Cooking with cultured butter produces much more intense flavours and in particular makes rather good biscuits!

Cultured Buttermilk

Buttermilk is the by-product of butter churning. It is similar to skimmed milk but with a slightly acidic taste. It has traditionally been used in baking, and folklore has always considered a glass of raw buttermilk to be full of health benefits. You can buy cultured buttermilk in shops, but beware of commercially made versions, where lactic acid is added to skimmed milk.

Whey

Whey is the liquid part of the milk after curds, for cheese, have been made. You can also strain yogurt to make a whey. Soaking grains in whey reduces phytic acid and makes grains easier to digest. Whey is often used as a starter culture for lacto-fermented vegetables.

VEGETABLES

Traditionally vegetables were preserved at their seasonal peak and an infinite number of methods and traditions evolved around fermenting and preserving vegetables.

Sauerkraut

This well-known cabbage ferment is made by slicing, adding salt, pounding, packing into a jar and pressing down well so that the cabbage is submerged under liquid. Once submerged, the cabbage is left to ferment. Do not buy sauerkraut that's been made with vinegar or is pasteurized, as it will be missing the important health benefits.

Kimchi

Kimchi is another well-known vegetable ferment and in Korea, where kimchi originated, it is generally eaten at every meal. Kimchi is made by first brining vegetables, then fermenting with spices, chilli, ginger and garlic, often with the addition of seafood ingredients, such as fermented anchovy sauce and salted shrimp.

Top left: Buttermilk; Top right: Sauerkraut; Bottom: Kimchi

Traditional Pickles

Traditional vegetable pickles are naturally fermented by the action of lactic bacteria and are a rich source of beneficial bacteria and enzymes. The use of vinegar for pickling does not produce the same nourishing food (so, if buying, look for the fermented kind if you want the nutritional benefits). Pickled small cucumbers known as sour dill pickles are the most widely recognized vegetable pickle, but you can pickle a whole medley of vegetables. The term 'pickle' is often used to collectively describe any fermented vegetable.

LEGUMES

Probably because its digestibility is particularly improved by the process, the best-known fermented legume is the soybean, which is used to make the traditional Eastern ferments: soy sauce, miso, natto and tempeh.

Soy Sauce

Soy sauce is a liquid usually made from soybeans, wheat, water and salt. Soy sauce is fermented and aged, traditionally in wooden casks, for up to two years. Japanese tamari is made without the addition of wheat, but possibly a little rice wine is added instead. There are light and dark soy sauces, and generally the Chinese sauces are thicker than the Japanese ones. Today many soy sauces found in shops are chemically produced. They are made over a couple of days by hydrolysing soy protein and combining with other flavourings. They have none of the true flavours and undertones of traditionally fermented soy sauces.

Miso

Traditionally, Japanese miso is made by combining koji with cooked soybeans, salt and water, then leaving the mixture to ferment. Koji is a starter culture made from incubating steamed grains with the mould Aspergillus oryzae. By varying the kind of

koji (it can be made from barley, rice or wheat), along with the proportion of ingredients and the duration of the ageing process, many varieties as well as different regional styles of miso are made. Broadly speaking, there are two main groups of miso, sweet and dark. Sweet miso is beige or yellow in colour and made using high proportions of koji. This kind of miso has a short fermentation period of up to eight weeks. Dark miso is salty, has a lower koji content and a much longer fermentation period, usually around 2–3 years. It has various names including red miso and barley miso. When choosing a miso search out a traditionally fermented and unpasteurized variety.

Natto

Natto is made from soybeans fermented with the bacteria Bacillus natto, which grows abundantly on rice straw. Natto are found in China, Korea and Thailand. For many people the slimy mucilaginous coating on the beans is unappetizing, though of course for many people it is quite delicious!

Tempeh

Indonesian tempeh is made from soybeans fermented with the mould Rhizopus oligosporus. Mould ferments require oxygen, so unlike other ferments it is an aerobic fermentation. Tempeh can also be made with other legumes and you can also combine the legume with grains, such as wheat, millet and rice. To succeed at making tempeh you need to produce an environment of the right moisture and heat – easy if you live in Indonesia! Once you have established a suitable incubation chamber the rest of the process is simple and the end result far more delicious than any frozen or jar varieties you will find ready-made to buy.

GRAINS

All over the world where grains are grown, traditionally, they have been fermented to produce porridge, gruels, breads and beverages. The fermentation process makes grains more nutritious and easier to digest.

Natto

Sourdough Bread

The best-known grain ferment is sourdough bread. This kind of bread is fermented with the help of wild yeasts. These wild yeasts are unique to different environments, including your kitchen, and climate. Mixing a wild yeast culture into flour and water to make bread creates bubbles causing the bread to rise, and the lactic acid ferment gives the bread its characteristic sour taste. Other grain ferments include fermented buckwheat breads and pancakes, idlis, fermented dosas and uttapams.

FRUITS

There are different types of fruit ferments including wines and chutneys. The best-known traditional fermented fruit is most likely the Japanese pickled ume plum, or 'umeboshi'.

Umeboshi

An ancient Japanese medicinal food, umeboshi are unique in their flavour: tart, tangy and salty – a taste-bud sensation. Umeboshi plums as well as an umeboshi paste made from the plum are both easy to source and add zest to any dish. The pickling juice from the plums can be bought separately as umeboshi plum vinegar.

VINEGAR

The first vinegars were probably discovered by accident – an unintended outcome of making alcohol. Vinegars can be made from the exposure of beer, wine and cider to Acetobacter bacteria. By far the most popular vinegar to make at home for its health benefits and pleasing taste is apple cider vinegar.

Apple Cider Vinegar

Apple cider vinegar has a long tradition of being a health tonic. If you buy apple cider vinegar, make sure it is unpasteurized, bottled in glass and preferably with a 'mother' – the acetic acid 'mat' (a bacterial growth) that helps turn the cider into vinegar.

BEVERAGES

Fermented beverages have a long history and there is a wide range of flavours to be found, from simple lacto-ferments to the more complex flavours of alcohol ferments.

Water Kefir

Water kefir is a fermented beverage made with water kefir grains, which are gelatinous microorganisms. Water kefir can be flavoured with herbs, fruits and spices. It is very easy to make and is a good source of beneficial bacteria.

Kombucha

Kombucha, a fermented black tea, has in recent years become a very popular drink. It is made from a specific culture known as a SCOBY – symbiotic 'colony' of bacteria and yeast. This gelatinous community of microorganisms, also referred to as a 'mother', ferments a mixture of black tea and sugar into a tart, slightly fizzy (marginally alcoholic) drink.

Wine

Wine is a beverage made from the fermentation of fruit. In general, we think of wine being made from grapes. Grape variety, soil, climate and local yeast cultures, collectively known as terroir, determine the unique flavours of different wine varieties.

Top: Apple cider vinegar; Bottom left: Water kefir.

Mead

In a very short time, honey diluted with water will ferment and turn into mead. A mead that contains spices or herbs is called a metheglin.

Beer

Beer is one of the oldest beverages known and is an alcoholic ferment generally made from barley, hops, water and yeast.

MEATS

Raw fermented meat products have been produced for centuries in different regions of the world. One of the main targets during fermentation and ripening of salamis and hams is the reduction of water and prevention of the growth of harmful bacteria, so temperature and humidity control is vital.

Salami

The meat for salami is mixed with salt and spices, often inoculated with a special culture, and then allowed to cure naturally, without additives. Meat is extremely susceptible to microbial damage and the process of fermentation was traditionally used to suppress the growth of harmful organisms.

Ham

There are many fermented raw hams, including Jamón Serrano from Spain, Prosciutto di Parma from Italy, Kraški pršut from Slovenia, Jambon de Bayonne from France and Virginia ham in the United States. While fermented meats like salamis and hams are a good method of preservation, they do not have the same health-giving properties as lacto-fermented vegetables and dairy products.

MUCH-LOVED FLAVOURS

The intrinsic flavour of some of our most loved foods comes from fermentation, including coffee, vanilla, chocolate and olives.

Coffee

Coffee beans are fermented to ease the removal of a layer of mucilage from the seed. This process influences the flavour of the finished bean.

Vanilla

Vanilla pods (beans) are dried for 24–36 hours, blanched in hot water, then fermented before drying.

Chocolate

The fermenting process is specifically used to develop the flavour of the cacao bean and is an important step in chocolate production.

Olives

Olives are one of the most important food ferments. The fermentation process makes the olives more digestible and reduces the bitterness and toxicity of phenol compounds.

TOOLS & EQUIPMENT

One of the advantages of fermentation is that, in general, you do not require a lot of specialized equipment, but there are some basic tools that will make the process easier.

VESSELS

First, you will need a selection of vessels: bowls for preparation and jars or crocks in which to ferment your produce. All over the world, all manner of vessels have been used for fermentation, from gourds to pits. The traditional earthenware pots called onggi were the famous Korean kimchi vessels and oke, cedar wood vats, were traditionally used to ferment miso. You too might like to use a variety of fermenting vessels, but if you are just beginning your fermenting journey, the best fermentation vessels for you to use are glass jars – they are easy to keep clean and you can clearly see how your ferment is progressing.

Glass Vessels

Glass is a good option for fermenting vegetables and many dairy products. It's easy to see the fermenting material and monitor its progress. Recycled bottles and jars are readily available for small batches of fermented vegetables, or it is well worth buying a selection of sizes of Mason or Kilner jars. Wide-mouthed litre/gallon 'pickle' jars are also worth buying, as they are relatively inexpensive and easy to source online. Glass demijohns are ideal for making wine, mead and carbonated drinks. NB: make sure all glass jars are scrupulously clean and sterilized before use.

Ceramic Vessels

Ceramic, made from clay, is fired at a high temperature and includes earthenware and porcelain. There are many different ceramic containers that you can use for

fermentation. It is also possible to buy ceramic fermenting crocks designed specifically for fruit and vegetable lacto-fermentation. They come with a pair of ceramic discs which, when positioned, keep the ingredients submerged. The Harsch crock made by the German Sudkeramic ceramic company is a good choice. The crock uses a V-shaped gutter in which the lid sits. The gutter is filled with water to provide a seal while gas bubbles out. The crock comes with weighing stones to keep vegetables submerged.

Plastic Vessels

Technically, plastic can be used for fermentation, but it is not a good choice. Many harmful chemicals can leach from the plastic into your ferment, and plastic is relatively easily damaged – cracks and scratches can harbour undesirable microorganisms. However, you may feel safer using plastic bottles for carbonated beverages to eliminate the attentive monitoring necessary of a glass bottle to prevent the potential risk of an explosion!

Above left: A fermentation crock with weights. Above: Bottles with breathable cloth 'lids'

Lids

Ferments need protecting from flies, but at the same time gases must be able to escape. You can cover with cloth, such as muslin (cheesecloth), which is secured with a rubber band or string. The cloth will keep pests out and at the same time allow a way out for the gas by-products of fermentation. Tight-fitting jar lids are an option, but need daily attention to loosen the lid and reduce the build-up of gas. It is possible to buy a variety of lids with fitted airlocks to seal the jar, which allow gas to escape.

BASIC TOOLS

Knives and Chopping Tools

A good sharp chef's knife is essential. Choose good-quality, stainless-steel-bladed knives as they are resistant to rusting, though they can stain

Above: A demijohn with fermenting alcohol and airlock

if over-exposed to salt water or vinegar. Make sure knives are washed well and dried after use. Vegetables can be sliced or chopped. A mandolin can be useful and, if you go into large-scale production, a food processor will be a great help.

Chopping Board

A large wooden chopping board is perfect for vegetable preparation.

Pounding Tool

A flat-ended wooden rolling pin is ideal as a pounding tool, which is helpful when making vegetable ferments that need to ferment in their own juices.

Wooden Spoons

Metal is considered to be damaging to some kinds of cultures, namely kefir and Kombucha, so it's easy to adopt the habit of only using wooden spoons for all ferments and keeping a set of wooden spoons of different sizes especially for this purpose.

Weights

Keeping vegetables submerged during fermentation is essential. A smooth stone, sterilized in boiling water for 5 minutes, a glass jar filled with water or a bought ceramic fermentation weight are all good options.

Kitchen Towels & Tea Towels

These come in useful to throw over vegetables soaking in brine overnight and for insulating jars that may need to be warmer than room temperature.

Strainer

A strainer is particularly useful, especially for straining out kefir grains and separating vegetables from brine. It is suggested that you should only use a plastic one, but a good-quality stainless-steel strainer is fine providing you strain quickly and do not leave any kefir grains sitting in it. Prolonged contact between acidic ferments and most metal causes corrosion. Good-quality, solid stainless steel will resist corrosion.

Grater

Sometimes you can introduce a different texture to your ferments by grating vegetables instead of slicing or chopping, so it's handy to have a grater.

SPECIALIZED EQUIPMENT

If you are going to start fermenting a large quantity of vegetables it is worth investing in a couple of large ceramic crocks, and there are a whole range of beautiful designs to choose from.

Digital Thermometer & Incubation Chamber

Legume fermentation often requires extra equipment. Tempeh, for example, needs to be held at a specific temperature, with a certain humidity, for a minimum of 24 hours; so a digital thermometer will come in handy. An incubation chamber is a must for making tempeh; there are methods to adapt refrigerators and aquariums, but a dehydrator can also be used for this purpose.

Grain Mill

Once you start making your own sourdough breads you may like to grind your own flour, in which case you will need a grain mill. You can buy either a hand grinding mill or an electric one.

Idli Steamer

Making idli requires an idli steamer. It is pretty hard to improvise and a three-tray stainless steel steamer is cheap. They are easy to use – just insert the steamer over boiling water and the perforations in the little cups allow the idli to steam.

Yogurt-maker

Though not absolutely necessary you may choose to buy a yogurt-maker, as they can be helpful for accurate temperature control.

Making Wines or Fruit Drinks

If you start making alcoholic beverages you will need demijohns, a siphon and possibly a hydrometer to measure the specific gravity so you can discover the alcohol potential. A large stainless-steel saucepan 5.5 litres/10 pints will also be essential if you need to bring infusing herbs or fruit to the boil.

Top: Idlis in a steamer tray; Bottom left: A yogurt-maker; Bottom right: Testing the alcohol

BASIC PRINCIPLES & PREPARATION

Through observation and more recently through an increasing knowledge of microbes, we have honed our understanding of the fermentation processes, of which there are three basic types: lactic, ethyl alcohol and acetic fermentations. Preparing ferments is relatively simple, but there are a few basic principles and techniques that are worth understanding and these will help guide you on your fermentation journey.

ORGANIC

Ultimately your ferment will only be as good as the ingredients you start with, so try to begin with the best. Organic food comes from a natural system that supports a healthy balance of microorganisms and do not allow chemical pesticides, which potentially can stop the growth of essential bacteria when you ferment. Research has shown there are more nutrients, especially minerals and phyto-nutrients, in organic food, so by choosing organic your ferments will be brimming with nutrition.

SALT

Salt is an important ingredient in many ferments, as it helps check the growth of unwanted bacteria and slows down the fermentation process, allowing full-bodied flavours to develop. The best salt to use is an unrefined sea salt or rock salt, as both contain a broad spectrum of trace elements. Look for specks of colour in your salt – grey, pink or black – as this shows the minerals have not been removed. Good choices of unrefined sea salt include Cornish sea salt and Celtic sea salt, and a good choice of unrefined rock salt is Himalayan pink salt. Do not use a refined table salt, which has all the trace elements removed, the addition of an anti-caking agent and possibly iodine.

Variety of different sea salts: black and red Hawaiian, grey Celtic, pink Himalayan, flaky Murray River Australian

Why Salt is Used in Fermentation

Salt is used in the fermentation process for a number of reasons:

- To inhibit unwanted microbes, while allowing lactobacilli, which are reasonably tolerant of salt, to thrive
- To pull the water out of vegetables so they can ferment in their own juices
- To keep vegetables crisp by slowing down the enzymes that cause vegetables to go mushy
- To prevent mould
- To enhance flavour

There are two different techniques of incorporating salt into your ferment, either as dry salt or as a brine. Throughout this book fine grain salt has been used.

WATER

Tap water often has chlorine added to it to kill microorganisms, so you need to use filtered water or to boil the water. Alternatively, you can leave the water in a container with a large surface area for 24 hours and most chlorine will evaporate. If chloramines, which are created by adding ammonia to chlorine, have been added to your water they can only be removed by filtering, so check with your water company to see how your water is treated. Mineral content of water varies, which may have a bearing on your ferments: lacto-fermented vegetables are generally not affected, a high mineral content is perfect for water kefir, but Kombucha prefers a less mineral-rich water.

NB: When a recipe in this book calls for water for the main ferment, it is assumed that it is filtered, boiled or evaporated as described here.

LACTO-FERMENTATION

Various strains of Lactobacillus bacteria are responsible for lacto-fermentation. All you need to do is create the right environment for these microorganisms to flourish. The basic process of a lacto-fermentation is straightforward and can either be left to a wild fermentation or more controlled with a cultured fermentation.

A wild fermentation is one that occurs spontaneously from the Lactobacillus bacteria that are all around. The bacteria digest sugar from the fermentation substrate and in the process create lactic acid.

A cultured fermentation is helped by adding specific bacteria to aid the fermentation. Some lacto-ferments, for example kefir and Kombucha, will not happen spontaneously but rely on a culture being added.

Grating and salting cabbage for sauerkraut

Fermenting Vegetables

Given the right conditions, lacto-fermentation of vegetables will happen naturally because of the Lactobacillus bacteria living on the vegetables.

After the chosen vegetables are prepared, salt is added either by soaking in a brine for 12 hours then draining, or by mixing with dry salt and pounding. Root crops work well with the brine method and cabbages and other leaves work well with dry salting, but methods and traditions vary. It is possible to make lacto-fermented vegetables without salt, but this can result in mushy vegetables and mould.

Once the vegetables are ready, they are tightly packed into the chosen vessel. It is important to ensure all air bubbles are pressed out and the vegetables are fully submerged, as the lactic acid bacteria grow in an anaerobic environment. The more you press the more liquid will come out, so if there is not enough liquid add a little brine, then weight it down and leave to ferment.

Packing and weighting the jar, and the finished sauerkraut

BORAGE
VINEGAR

Leave for five days, then taste. Keep tasting until the right degree of acidity has been reached for your palate and the bubbles have subsided. The time this takes will vary depending on the amount of salt used and the temperature of the environment – a few days to a number of weeks.

Ideally an initial temperature of 21°C/70°F starts the fermentation, then cooler, about 18°C/65°F and finally store in a cool, dry place of about 10°C/50°F where the flavours will continue to develop. Once the jar is opened store in the refrigerator, or if you have made a large crock, in a cool place.

Though not necessary some people, for whatever reason, prefer to speed up or have greater control over the process with the addition of a bacterial culture. Whey is the most common starter culture for vegetables. Some people ferment entirely in whey. Using whey is obviously not suitable for people who avoid dairy. Dried bacteria strains can also be bought and used to ferment vegetables.

DAIRY

Fermented milk products evolved using raw milk. It is possible to source raw organic milk and cream so, if you are able to, it's worth using it. The plentiful supply of lactic bacteria in raw milk will enable the milk to sour naturally into curds and whey, while pasteurized milk requires a starter. If you cannot source raw organic milk, use whole pasteurized milk, but do not use UHT milk. See pages 106–16 for full dairy and kefir recipes.

Making Yogurt

The basic technique for making yogurt, whether the milk is raw or pasteurized, is to heat the milk to 82°C/180°F, then cool to 43°C/110°F before adding a culture and leaving in a warm place for 8–12 hours. The culture can either be a bought powdered culture made up of specific bacteria or a spoonful of bought live yogurt.

Making Yogurt Cheese

To make a yogurt cheese, strain the yogurt through muslin (cheesecloth) set over a strainer or colander for 12 hours. The whey can be used in baking and makes good pancakes and breads.

Making Milk Kefir

This kefir uses a starter culture of grains, but the milk does not need to be heated before the grains are added. The kefir grains feed on the lactose (sugar) in the milk.

MAKING KOMBUCHA

This is a lacto-fermented dairy-free drink made from sweet black tea and a Kombucha 'mother'.

Above left: Yogurt cheese; Above: Kombucha

The beneficial bacteria and yeasts that make up kefir grains and the Kombucha 'mother' both need sugar to live and reproduce. You cannot make either drink without sugar, but very little is left in the final product. The best sugar to use is an unrefined cane sugar. Be careful about substituting honey for sugar, as honey has antimicrobial properties, which can weaken the ferment.

ALCOHOL FERMENTS

Alcoholic fermentation is the conversion of sugar into alcohol and carbon dioxide by yeast. Malted grains are made into beer, rice into sake, grapes into wine, cassava into kasiri, apples into cider and honey into mead.

Alcoholic fermentation can be a wild fermentation or the wild yeasts can be killed and a commercial yeast strain added for a more controlled ferment.

Fermenting Fruits & Herbs

Fermenting fruits and herbs into alcoholic beverages can be simple. Place your chosen fruit in a bowl, pour on boiling water and mash well. Cover and leave for three days, stirring each day. Strain through a wine bag and combine with a sugar syrup and any herbs or spices. Add a commercial wine yeast, pour into a demijohn, fit with an airlock and leave to ferment for three months. Syphon into a clean demijohn and leave for another three months before bottling.

Kombucha is often a slightly alcoholic drink – potentially up to 3% alcohol depending on the length of fermentation. Commercial brands are meant to limit alcohol content to 0.5% – this often means pasteurisation, which takes away the health benefits.

ACETIC ACID FERMENT

Acetic acid is produced by fermenting alcohol with Acetobacter bacteria to make vinegar. All vinegars from different alcoholic beverages are made in the same way, by exposure to air, as acetic acid fermentation is an aerobic process.

Making Vinegar

To make your own vinegar, pour your chosen alcohol into a bowl with a large surface area, cover with muslin (cheesecloth) and depending on alcohol content, temperature and aeration, the vinegar will be ready in about a month. You may notice a bloom appearing on the surface – this is a vinegar 'mother' – a mat of acetic bacteria which can be transferred to your next batch as a starter.

BASIC RECIPES

BRINE

This is a basic brine used for fermenting firm vegetables or dill pickles. Remember to use unrefined fine grain sea or rock salt.

Makes about 2.25 litres / 4 pints / 9½ cups

6 tbsp salt
2.25 litres/4 pints/9½ cups water

Combine the salt and water in a jar and stir until dissolved. Store in a cool, dark place in any glass jar sealed with a lid, for up to 3 months.

LEAVEN

Here is a method to make a sourdough starter or leaven. Any grain-based flour will make a sourdough starter, but the easiest sourdough starter to maintain is probably a rye, so the following recipe is for a rye sourdough starter. Make sure the water you use is not chlorinated, as bacteria and yeasts will not flourish if the water has chlorine in it.

DAY 1 Add 50 ml/2 fl oz/¼ cup water and 2 tablespoons rye flour to a 750 ml/1¼ pint glass jar. Stir the flour and water together with a clean spoon, cover with muslin (cheesecloth) and loosely close the jar lid. Leave at room temperature (about 20°C/68°F) away from direct sunlight for 24 hours.

DAY 2 Add 50 ml /2 fl oz/¼ cup water and 2 tablespoons rye flour to the jar, stir well and leave 24 hours.

DAY 3 Add 50 ml/2 fl oz/¼ cup water and 2 tablespoons rye flour to the jar, stir well and leave 24 hours.

DAY 4 By now, you should notice bubbles on the surface of the batter, but do not worry if this has not happened – it may just be slow. Add 50 ml/2 fl oz/¼ cup water and 2 tablespoons rye flour to the jar, stir well and leave again.

DAY 5 Discard half of the batter and to the remainder stir in 100 g/3½ oz/scant 1 cup rye flour and enough water to make a thick batter.

DAY 6 By now your leaven should be active and have developed a fruity smell. Double the quantity of batter using rye flour and water (just judge this by eye) and leave for 24 hours.

DAY 7   START USING & MAINTAINING YOUR LEAVEN

Every time you use some of the leaven to make bread, double the quantity that remains with rye flour and water. Mix vigorously and leave in a warm place for 12 hours before storing in the refrigerator. Your sourdough starter can live for ever and be passed down from generation to generation. It needs attention, but if you go away it can be stored for up to a month in the refrigerator. If looking a bit sad, coax it back to life with warmth and food.

IDLI, DOSA & UTTAPAM BATTER

Idli, dosa and uttapam can be made from the same basic fermented batter. Idli are small steamed cakes, dosa are thin fried pancakes and uttapam are thicker pancakes made with vegetables cooked in the batter.

Makes 750 ml/1¼ pints/3¼ cups

450 g/1 lb/2¼ cups idli rice or basmati rice
150 g/5 oz/¾ cup lentils (traditionally uses white lentils but works fine with
  split red lentils)
1 tsp salt

Soak the rice and lentils separately in plenty of water overnight.

Next day, drain the lentils, put in a blender, add water and blend, adding enough water until you have a fairly thick, smooth batter. Transfer to a bowl.

Drain the rice, put in the blender, add the salt and blend with enough water to make a just pourable consistency. Add to the lentil mixture and whisk together for 2 minutes until the mixture is well aerated.

Pour the batter into a jar large enough to allow plenty of room for expansion. Cover and leave in a warm place for 24 hours, or until well risen and bubbly, then use.

SAUERKRAUT

A classic vegetable ferment, sauerkraut can be used as a side, or in a variety
of recipes.

*Makes about 3.5 litres/6 pints to fill 2–3 large glass jars equivalent
4 litres/7 pints/1 gallon capacity or 1 large crock*

2.25 kg/5 lb white cabbage heads, shredded
3 tbsp sea salt

Place the cabbage in a large metal bowl. Sprinkle over 1 tablespoon salt and pound
with a rolling pin until the juices starts to flow. Cover with a cloth and leave overnight.

Next day, place about 5 cm/2 inch cabbage into 2–3 glass jars or a large crock and
press firmly down. Sprinkle with a little salt and repeat until full.

Firmly compress the cabbage layers leaving space at the top of the jar. Place a small
plate or an outside cabbage leaf over the cabbage, then place a weight on top. Push
the cabbage down gently so it is submerged. If there is not enough brine to cover it,
make a little more (*see* page 90). Cover with a cloth.

Leave to stand at room temperature. Check the sauerkraut stays under the brine and
top up if necessary. After a week, the cabbage will most likely have fermented enough
to be eaten, but you can leave it for another 2–3 weeks before securing with a lid and
storing in a cool, dry place. Leave for up to 6 months; both the flavour and texture will
change during this period as the kraut continues to develop. Once opened, store in the
refrigerator and consume within 6 weeks.

ROOT VEG KIMCHI

This legendary ferment from Korea livens up any dish from salads to soups to risotto. It is quite potent so can scent the refrigerator somewhat, so you can store instead in a cool, dry place. This version uses root vegetables.

Makes about 1 litre/ 1³/₄ pints/ 4 cups

750 g/1½ lb root vegetables, such as turnips, carrots, mouli (daikon)
   and Jerusalem artichokes, peeled and finely sliced
1 litre/1¾ pints/4 cups brine (*see* page 90)
3 tbsp grated ginger
4 garlic cloves, peeled and chopped
2 chillies, chopped whole or seeded

Place all the vegetables with the brine in a large bowl and leave overnight.

Put the spices in a mortar and pound with a pestle into a paste. Alternatively, use a food processor.

Drain the vegetables and reserve the brine. Mix the vegetables with the spice paste and pack into 1 litre/1¾ pint/34 oz clean jar. Press tightly down until the brine rises. If necessary, add some of the reserved brine so the liquid comes up over the vegetables. Weigh the vegetables down, cover with a cloth and leave in a warm place for a week. Seal with a lid, refrigerate and consume within 6 weeks

TEMPEH

Tempeh is traditionally made with soybeans, which are often hard to digest, but the fermentation process produces a firm-textured, easy-to-digest, protein-rich food. Tempeh works well with any legume, but peas are especially good.

Makes 500 g/1 lb 2 oz block

500 g/1 lb 2 oz/3½–3¾ cups dried peas or beans
2½ tbsp apple cider vinegar
1½ tsp tempeh starter (you can buy this online)

Soak the beans overnight.

Next day, drain and cook them until slightly underdone. Strain and pat dry with a towel.

Pulse the beans in a food processor to break up, but keep some whole to retain a satisfying texture. Transfer to a bowl and leave to cool to body temperature. Alternatively, crush the beans with a flat-ended rolling pin.

Add the vinegar and mix, then add the tempeh starter and mix thoroughly. Place into two small ziplock plastic bags (about 180 x 220 mm/7–8½ inch) that you have poked holes in with a skewer and incubate at 29–32°C (84–90°F) for 24 hours. Keep an eye on the temperature, as the process generates its own heat. A cohesive mat will form and eventually patches of grey will appear near the holes.

Remove from the incubator, cool to room temperature, then refrigerate and consume within 2 days or freeze for up to 2 months.

DASHI

While this mushroom-based stock is not fermented, it is included here as it forms the basis of the classic Japanese miso soup, which is made from the unique ferment miso. Dashi can be used whenever a recipe calls for stock.

Makes about 1.25 litres/2¼ pints/5¼ cups

1 piece kombu seaweed
6 shiitake mushrooms
1.5 litres/2½ pints/6⅓ cups water

Place the kombu, mushrooms and water in a pan and soak for at least 1 hour, then slowly bring to the boil. Reduce the heat and simmer for 10 minutes.

Strain and set the kombu and shiitake aside to use in another dish. Store the dashi in the fridge in glass jars for up to a week.

WHEY

This is a good alternative to making whey if you do not have access to raw milk.

Makes 300 ml/½ pint/1¼ cups whey and 300 g/11 oz cheese

600 ml/1 pint/2½ cups plain live yogurt (not Greek-style yogurt)

Drape a square of muslin (cheesecloth) over a bowl and pour the yogurt into the middle. Gather up the sides of the cloth, fasten securely with string, hang on a hook above the bowl and allow to drip into the bowl for 24 hours.

Transfer the whey collected in the bowl to a jar, seal with a lid and store in the refrigerator for up to 6 weeks. The soft cream cheese that remains can be used in much the same way as any cream cheese.

You can also make whey from raw milk. Place 600 ml/1 pint/2½ cups raw milk in a glass bowl and leave to stand at room temperature for 2 days until it separates, then continue as above.

YOGURT

Once you have started making your own yogurt, reserve a couple of tablespoons each time to start the next batch.

Makes about 1 litre/ 1³/₄ pints/ 4 cups

1 litre/1¾ pints/4 cups whole milk
2 rounded tbsp plain live yogurt as a starter culture

Heat the milk gently in a pan to 43°C/109°F. Remove from the heat and whisk in the yogurt.

If you are using a yogurt-maker, follow the maker's instructions.

Alternatively, pour the mixture into a Kilner or Mason jar, loosely fit the lid, cover in a dish towel for insulation and leave in a warm place for 8–12 hours. An ideal temperature would be 35°C/95°F. Store in the fridge for up to 2 weeks.

DAIRY MILK KEFIR

First you will need to source your milk kefir grains. Once you have them, use regularly and they will last indefinitely. You will also have plenty to share around with your friends and family or you can eat them.

Makes 600 ml/1 pint/2½ cups

1 tbsp milk kefir grains
600 ml/1 pint/2½ cups whole milk

Place the grains into a clean glass jar and pour in the milk. If this is your first batch and the grains are small, use half the quantity of milk to give the grains plenty of nourishment and encourage them to grow.

Loosely cover the jar and leave for 12–24 hours, stirring occasionally with a wooden spoon. The milk will become thick and effervescent. If the room is very warm, sometimes only 6–8 hours is required. You will need to experiment, but you are aiming for thick, sour-tasting yogurt.

Strain the kefir through a clean plastic strainer and collect the grains. You can either drink it immediately or chill first. After some time in the refrigerator, the kefir milk becomes creamier in texture. Store in the refrigerator for up to 2 weeks.

Place the strained grains into a clean jar and repeat the process with fresh milk. Alternatively, the grains can be stored in the refrigerator in a little fresh milk. If looked after correctly, the grains will probably double in size within two weeks of constant use.

ALMOND MILK KEFIR

An alternative kefir for those who avoid dairy.

Makes 1 litre/1³/₄ pints/4 cups

175 g/6 oz/generous 1 cup skinned whole almonds, soaked for 24 hours

900 ml/1½ pints/3¾ cups water

4 dates, soaked for 12 hours

good pinch salt

1 tbsp milk kefir grains

Blend the almonds, water, dates and salt in a high-speed blender until smooth. Strain through muslin (cheesecloth), squeezing well to remove excess liquid.

Pour the almond milk into a large glass jar, add the kefir grains and stir in with a wooden spoon. Cover with a cloth and leave in a warm place for 12–24 hours. The mixture will thicken and become tangy.

Strain the grains and store the almond kefir in a glass jar in the refrigerator for up to a week. It will separate out, but stir or shake it back together.

VARIATION You can also make almond milk kefir without straining, in which case, tie the kefir grains loosely in muslin (cheesecloth) before immersing in the almond milk. The finished product will be a little grainy.

WATER KEFIR

An easy-to-make sparkling, refreshing drink full of health benefits

Makes 600 ml/1 pint/2½ cups

600 ml/1 pint/2½ cups water

2 tbsp unrefined cane sugar

1 tsp molasses (optional, but adds minerals)

4 dried figs

3 slices fresh ginger

3 slices lemon

2 tbsp water kefir grains

Place the water, sugar and molasses (if using) into a jar and stir well to dissolve the sugar and molasses. Add the figs, ginger and lemon and stir well. Add the grains, then cover loosely with a lid or muslin (cheesecloth) secured with a rubber band. Leave at room temperature for 24–72 hours, depending on how zesty you want the finished kefir.

Strain the figs, ginger, lemon and grains. Store the kefir in flip-top or screw-top bottles in the fridge and drink within 2 to 3 days. Take care when opening the bottle in case of any build-up of pressure. Discard the figs, ginger and lemon. Store the grains in the refrigerator covered with water with a spoonful of sugar added for up to 10 days, or use again immediately.

APPLE CIDER VINEGAR

Here is a method to make health-promoting apple cider vinegar from scratch. You can also make it from any bought organic cider.

5 sweet apples, such as Jonagold, Gala or Fuji, washed and chopped
  into medium pieces
1 tbsp unrefined cane sugar
enough filtered water to cover

Place the apples and sugar in a large, wide-necked jar and cover with water. Place muslin (cheesecloth) over the jar and secure with a rubber band. Leave in a warm, dark place for about 2 weeks. It will bubble and foam as the sugars begin to ferment. Gently push down any pieces of apple that rise to the top.

After 2 weeks, the apple pieces will fall to the bottom of the jar. Strain and discard the apple. Return the liquid to the same jar and cover it again. Return to a warm, dark place and it will transform over the next 4–6 weeks into vinegar with an acetic mat on the top known as a 'mother'.

You can tell by the taste when the vinegar is ready. You do not want it to taste alcoholic – it should be pleasantly acidic. Strain and store in flip-top bottles in a cool, dark place where the vinegar will last indefinitely. Save the 'mother' to use on the next batch, as it will help speed up the process.

SALADS, SIDES
& CONDIMENTS

SAUERKRAUT WITH CARROTS

Any leftovers will last in the refrigerator for up to 5 days. Serve the dressing separately as it works well to keep a contrast between the simple salad and the dressing.

Serves 4

450 g/1 lb plain cabbage sauerkraut (*see* page 96)

300 g/11 oz carrots, peeled and cut into fine matchsticks

For the dressing:

1 tbsp raw apple cider vinegar (bought or homemade)

½ tsp raw honey

1 tsp mustard seeds

6 tbsp walnut oil

50 g/2 oz/scant ½ cup roughly chopped walnuts

1 garlic clove, peeled and crushed

½ tsp freshly chopped thyme

Holding it over a bowl, squeeze the juice from the sauerkraut, then place the sauerkraut into a separate bowl.

Toss the carrots in the sauerkraut juice and leave to soften for 30 minutes.

Meanwhile, blitz all the ingredients for the dressing together and pour into a bowl.

Strain the carrots (save the juice to add to your next batch of sauerkraut or kimchi) and mix with the sauerkraut, then pile into another bowl. Serve the salad and dressing separately.

SAUERKRAUT SUSHI

This is a nourishing combination of nori seaweed and sauerkraut.

Serves 4

300 g/11 oz/1⅓ cups sushi rice

600 ml/1 pint/2½ cups water

1 tbsp rice vinegar

½ tsp honey

4 toasted nori sheets

6 tbsp sauerkraut (*see* page 96)

handful alfalfa sprouts

1 carrot, peeled and cut into matchsticks

1 tbsp grated horseradish

handful flat-leaf parsley, stems removed

soy sauce, to serve

Put the rice in a small pan with the water. Bring to the boil, reduce the heat and cook until the water is absorbed and the rice is tender. Stir through the vinegar and honey and leave to cool.

Lay a nori sheet on a sushi mat, shiny-side down. If you do not have a mat you can use greaseproof (wax) paper.

Cover with rice leaving a 1 cm/½ inch border at the top and bottom. Put a layer of sauerkraut over the rice, then alfalfa, carrot, horseradish and parsley.

Fold the bottom edge of the seaweed over the filling, then roll it up firmly. Dampen the top border with a little water to help seal the roll. Repeat to make four rolls. Unless you want to serve the sushi immediately, leave in the refrigerator for a few hours.

With a sharp knife, cut each roll into 5 or 6 pieces and serve with soy sauce for dipping.

SAUERKRAUT SALAD WITH APPLES & WALNUTS

Cabbage, apples and walnuts are a winning combination.

Serves 4

400 g/14 oz sauerkraut (*see* page 96)

1 red-skinned apple, quartered, cored and finely sliced

2 spring onions (scallions), diagonally sliced

1 small raddichio, coarsely shredded

175 g/6 oz/1¾ cups walnuts

2 tsp walnut oil

salt flakes and freshly ground black pepper

175 ml/6 fl oz/scant ¾ cup plain live yogurt

zest of 1 lemon

juice of ½ lemon

Put the sauerkraut in a bowl, add the apple, spring onions (scallions), radicchio, walnuts and walnut oil and mix together to combine. Divide between four serving dishes. Top each salad with a twist of black pepper and a few salt flakes.

Mix the yogurt, lemon juice and zest together in a small bowl and serve with the salad.

KIMCHI SALAD

A tangy salad bursting with kimchi flavours.

Serves 4

350 g/12 oz Chinese (Napa) cabbage, cut or torn into pieces,
    about 5 x 7.5 cm/2 x 3 inches
2 tsp salt
2 tsp chilli (red pepper) flakes
2 garlic cloves, peeled and finely chopped
thumb ginger, peeled and grated
1 tbsp fermented fish sauce (optional)
4 spring onions (scallions), cut into 7.5 cm/3 inch pieces

To serve:
1 tbsp toasted sesame oil
1 tsp sesame seeds

Place the cabbage in a large bowl, sprinkle with salt and rub into the leaves. Leave to soften for 30 minutes.

Rinse the cabbage and shake dry in a colander. Place the cabbage in another bowl, sprinkle over the pepper flakes, then add the garlic, ginger, fish sauce (if using) and spring onions (scallions), mix well and leave for 20 minutes.

Serve in bowls topped with the sesame oil and seeds.

VARIATION Alternatively, pile the cabbage into a jar and leave it at room temperature for 24 hours to gently begin to ferment.

TEMPEH SALAD WITH ROCKET, GLAZED APPLE & CRANBERRIES

This protein salad has a savoury, sweet and spicy kick.

Serves 2

200 g/7 oz tempeh (*see* page 100), cut into small cubes

1 red apple

25 g/1 oz ghee

4 handfuls rocket (arugula)

150 g/5 oz/1½ cups walnut pieces

100 g/3½ oz/scant 1 cup dried cranberries

juice of ½ lemon

2 tbsp hemp oil

1 tsp Dijon mustard

salt and freshly ground black pepper

For the marinade:

1 tbsp tamari

2 tsp grated ginger

2 tsp grated horseradish

1 tsp raw maple syrup

Place the tempeh in a bowl. Mix the marinade ingredients together, then pour over the tempeh and marinate for at least 1 hour.

Using an apple corer, remove the core and cut the apple into round slices, 5 mm/¼ inch thick.

Melt the ghee in a frying pan over a medium-high heat, add the apple and cook for 3 minutes before flipping over and cooking the other side. Transfer to a plate.

Pan-fry the tempeh until just beginning to caramelize.

Divide the rocket (arugula) between four plates and top with the apple, tempeh, walnuts and cranberries.

Mix the lemon juice, oil and mustard together, season well and spoon over the salad.

FERMENTED GREEN BEANS

Green beans are often pickled in vinegar. In the following recipe, a light lacto-fermentation makes them far more nutritious.

Makes two 1 litre/1³/₄ pint/34 oz jars

1 tsp chilli (red pepper) flakes

1 tsp mustard seeds

1 tsp white peppercorns

1 tsp coriander seeds

3 garlic cloves, peeled and sliced

450 g/1 lb/3⅓ cups French (green) beans or young runner (string) beans, tops removed

2.25 litres/4 pints/9½ cups brine (*see* page 90)

Divide all the spices and garlic between two 1 litre/1¾ pint/34 oz Kilner or Mason jars.

Place the beans in the jar, pressed together and standing upright, then cover the beans with the brine, leaving a little space at the top of each jar.

Cover with muslin (cheesecloth) or an airlock lid (*see* page 67) and leave in a warm place to culture. Once the right flavour and texture has been achieved – up to 2 weeks – seal with a secure lid and store in a cool place.

SOUR DILL PICKLES

Soaking the cucumber in cold water and adding vine (grape) leaves helps to keep your pickles crisp.

Makes 900 g/2 lb

900 g/2 lb pickling cucumbers
1 large bunch dill
1 onion, peeled and sliced
6 garlic cloves, peeled
1 tbsp black peppercorns
1 tbsp mustard seeds
3 vine (grape) leaves (optional)
1–1.5 litres/1¾–2½ pints/4–6⅓ cups brine (*see* page 90)

Soak the cucumbers in cold water for 2 hours.

Put the dill, onion, garlic, peppercorns and mustard seeds into a suitable jar or crock, then add the pickling cucumbers and vine (grape) leaves (if using).

Pour the brine into the jar until all the ingredients are covered, then place a weight on top to make sure the cucumbers stay submerged.

Leave to ferment in a warm place for at least 5 days but possibly up to 2 weeks. Taste them to make sure they are to your liking and once they are sour enough, store in the refrigerator and consume within a year.

MIXED PICKLES

Mixed pickles are a good way of using up seasonal gluts; most vegetables with the exception of ripe tomatoes and aubergine (eggplant) work well with this pickling method. This recipe is more about a method than exact quantities.

Makes… as much or as little as you want!

selection of vegetables, such as cauliflower florets, carrot slices, pepper slices, small whole radishes, beans, chopped celery and garlic cloves
spices, such as coriander seeds, peppercorns, bay leaf, rosemary sprigs
vine (grape) leaves (optional, but helps to keep pickles crisp)
brine (*see* page 90)

Place the vegetables, spices and vine (grape) leaves (if using) into wide-necked jars. Pour the brine over the vegetables, leaving 2.5 cm/1 inch space at the top of the jar. Place a weight on top to hold the vegetables under the brine. Cover the jar with muslin (cheesecloth) or some other form of lid and leave to stand at room temperature. If you use a fitted lid you will need to release it daily to allow gases to escape (*see* page 67). Sometimes a scum will appear on the top, so simply skim it off.

After about 10 days or when the pickles taste to your liking, transfer the jar to the refrigerator and consume within a year.

GUNDRUK

Making gundruk is a way of preserving green leaves, and is a technique used particularly in Nepal and Bhutan. One of the method's main distinctions is that it does not use salt.

Makes… as much or as little as you want!

Gather some fresh leaves – spinach or radish tops are ideal – and leave to wilt in the sun, turning daily for 3 days. Lack of sun may call for a little improvisation: on the windowsill or by the oven are possibilities.

Coarsely chop the leaves, put into a crock and crush to release their juices, pressing down on the leaves until they are all submerged. If there is not enough liquid, add some water. Salt helps pull water out of vegetables, so leaves fermented without salt require more bruising and pounding to produce enough liquid. Once the leaves are submerged, weigh down and leave to ferment in a warm place for a week.

Drain and place the leaves in the sun to dry. A dehydrator is a good alternative to the sun. Once the leaves are completely dry, store in an airtight container in a dry place for up to a year.

Gundruk is used particularly in soups when there are few green leaves to harvest.

NUKA BRAN PICKLES

Another ferment that is more about a method than exact measurements. If you can master the art of making these pickles, your effort will be well rewarded. Traditionally these pickles are made using rice bran, but you can use wheat bran just as successfully. The following is a guideline. You just need bran, salt and water, but the addition of garlic, ginger, kombu and chilli adds a depth of flavour.

Makes a couple of bowlfuls (weekly if maintained)

1.5 litres/2½ pints/6⅓ cups water
120 g/4¼ oz/½ cup salt
1 kg/2¼ lb/20 cups rice or wheat bran
garlic cloves
ginger slices
kombu sheet
chillies
cabbage wedges
suitable vegetables to pickle including cauliflower, fine beans, broccoli, kohlrabi, radish, asparagus and mangetout (snow peas); vegetables can be whole, halved, cubed or sliced

Choose a suitable wide-mouthed, lidded container to use and half fill with the water. Mix in the salt and bran, adding enough of the remaining water to make the consistency of soft sand. Make sure the bran is well hydrated and there are no dry spots.

Add the garlic, ginger, kombu, chillies and 2 cabbage wedges, then mix well and bury everything in the bran bed, which is called a nukadoka in Japanese. Using a small pastry brush or a clean cloth, wipe down the sides of your container, put the lid on and leave in a warm place.

For the next few days, mix the bed well with your hands. After 3 days, discard the cabbage and add 2 more wedges – the cabbage is helping to establish a rich Lactobacillus culture. On day 5, discard the cabbage and start adding a variety of vegetables to pickle. The native bacteria on the vegetables will further colonize the bed. Replace them daily, tasting them as you remove them until they taste right. This may take up to 2 weeks. You are after a slightly salty, sour and tangy flavour and a soft texture but still with a little crunch.

When you bury your vegetables, flatten the surface of the nukadoka with your hands and press lightly down to ensure your vegetables are in good contact with the bran.

When you remove the vegetables from the bran, lightly brush off the bran with a pastry brush, and you can also rinse them in cold water. Serve small vegetables whole and neatly slice larger ones. As salt will keep being removed with the pickled vegetables, add a little salt every time you add vegetables.

If your nukadoka becomes too liquid from absorbing water from the vegetables add more bran and salt – salt should be 12 per cent of the weight of the bran.

Once you have an active nukadoka, it can live for ever. If you go away, pop it in the refrigerator.

MISO PICKLES

Miso makes a very good medium in which to pickle; vary your pickling with different miso varieties.

275 g/10 oz red miso paste
3 tbsp sake
thumb ginger, peeled and grated
6 garlic cloves, peeled
prepared vegetables of your choice, such as thick carrot slices, mouli (daikon) slices, celeriac (celery root) wedges, beans, whole small beetroot (beets), radish slices, turnip slices and sprouts

Mix the miso, sake and ginger together.

In a small crock or a glass jar or container, layer the miso mixture with the garlic and vegetables, finishing with a layer of miso and making sure the vegetables are completely covered. Put on a lid and leave for 2 weeks until the vegetables are infused with the miso flavours and the miso has absorbed water from the vegetables.

Remove the pickles, and use as a side or in rice or other grain dishes. The miso can be turned into a delicious soup or reused with the addition of more miso for another pickling. Can be stored in the refrigerator for up to a couple of days.

MISO SALAD DRESSING

Keep a jar of this richly flavoured salty dressing in the refrigerator, ready to enliven greens and salads.

Makes enough to dress a salad for 4–6

small piece ginger, peeled and grated

60 g/2¼ oz miso paste

2 tbsp soy sauce

2 tbsp rice vinegar

2 tbsp sesame oil

1 tbsp snipped chives

Place all the ingredients, except the chives, in a bowl and whisk well together.

Stir in the snipped chives. Store in a small glass jar, in the refrigerator, for up to 2 weeks.

HOT CHILLI SAUCE

A rich, fiery, fermented sauce, which tastes so much better than vinegary
bought alternatives.

Makes about 1.1 litres / 2 pints / 4²/₃ cups

1.3 kg/3 1b chillies, such as habanero, stalks removed and coarsely chopped
6 garlic cloves, peeled and finely chopped
1 tbsp unrefined cane sugar
2 tsp salt
125 ml/4 fl oz/½ cup whey (*see* page 106)

Place all the ingredients in a food processor and blend to a smooth paste.

Fill a glass jar – a Kilner or Mason jar would be ideal – with the chilli paste
and leave it loosely covered with a lid or piece of muslin (cheesecloth) in
a warm place for about a week. When the bubbling subsides, pour the
sauce into clean flip-top bottles and store in the refrigerator, where it will
last for up to 3 months.

PRESERVED LEMONS

Properly fermented lemons are a wonderful condiment and once made will last for years.

Makes about 2.25 litres/4 pints/9½ cups

1.1 kg/2½ lb lemons
65 g/2½ oz/⅓ cup unrefined sea salt

Finely trim the ends off the lemons, then slice the lemons as if to quarter them, but stop before you reach the base so the lemon remains intact.

Put a layer of salt at the bottom of a crock or jar. Fill the inside of the lemons with salt, then layer them into the crock or jar. Pound the lemons down with the end of a rolling pin. The lemons will slowly soften and release their juices which will combine with the salt to make a brine. Continue to fill the crock or jar with lemons and pound until the jar is full and the lemons are submerged.

Cover with muslin (cheesecloth) and leave to ferment at room temperature for 2 weeks. Secure with a lid and store in a cool, dry place for up to a year.

LABNEH

You can either eat labneh fresh or marinated in a herb-infused oil.

Serves 4–6

500 ml/18 fl oz/2 cups plain whole yogurt or Greek yogurt

½ tsp finely grated lemon zest

3 tbsp chopped herbs, such as tarragon, parsley, chervil and chives

about 150 ml/¼ pint/⅔ cup good-quality extra-virgin olive oil

salt and freshly ground black pepper

black sesame seeds, to scatter

Drape a square of muslin (cheesecloth) over a strainer set over a bowl and pour the yogurt into the middle. Gather up the sides of the cloth and tie the ends together with the yogurt in the middle. Leave in the refrigerator or in a cool, dark place to drain for 48 hours.

Scrape the cheese away from the muslin (cheesecloth) and turn into a bowl. Save the whey for fermenting or baking.

Roll the labneh into little balls and place in a clean glass jar.

Whisk the lemon zest and herbs into the oil and season to taste. Pour the oil over the labneh, seal with a lid and store in the refrigerator for 2 weeks.

Serve in a small dish as they are, or with fresh herbs and a scattering of black sesame seeds.

DRINKS &
SMOOTHIES

BEETROOT KVASS

An inexpensive, earthy, probiotic beetroot tonic.

Makes about 1.7 litres / 3 pints / 7 cups

4 medium beetroot (beets), peeled and cut into 2.5 cm/1 inch pieces
1 tbsp salt
100 ml/3½ fl oz/⅓ cup whey (*see* page 106)

Put the beetroot (beets) into a 2.25 litre/4 pint/80 oz jar, sprinkle the salt onto the beetroot, add the whey and top up with water leaving a 5 cm/2 inch gap at the top. Stir well. Loosely fit a lid and leave in a cool, dark place for 2–5 days. When the kvass is effervescent, transfer to the refrigerator and drink within 3 days.

CUCUMBER & KEFIR SMOOTHIE

This drink is refreshing, especially poured over ice cubes on a
hot summer day.

Makes 2 glasses

500 ml/18 fl oz/2 cups milk kefir (*see* page 110)

2 medium cucumbers, chopped, plus extra to garnish

½ avocado, peeled and chopped

12 mint leaves, plus extra to garnish

¼ tsp ground cumin

freshly ground black pepper

Place all the ingredients into a blender and blend well until smooth.
Divide between 2 glasses and top with a flourish of cucumber and
mint and a sprinkling of black pepper.

BLUEBERRY SMOOTHIE

A creamy and delicious probiotic drink. If using frozen blueberries there is no need to thaw them before using.

Makes 1–2 glasses

1 banana, peeled and chopped

150 ml/¼ pint/⅔ cup almond milk kefir (*see* page 112)

150 ml/¼ pint/⅔ cup plain live yogurt

125 g/4 oz/scant 1 cup blueberries (fresh or frozen)

Place all the ingredients into a blender and blend well until smooth. Pour into 1–2 glasses, garnish with fresh blueberries if liked, and drink immediately.

PROBIOTIC LEMONADE

An easy-to-make, healthy, tangy lemonade.

Makes about 900 ml/ 1½ pints/ 3¾ cups

juice of 6 lemons

125 g/4 oz/scant ⅔ cup unrefined cane sugar

125 ml/4 fl oz/½ cup whey (*see* page 106)

lemon slices, to serve

Put the lemon juice, sugar and whey with a little water in the bottom of a wide-mouthed jar, such as a Kilner or Mason jar, and stir until the sugar dissolves. Fill up with water, leaving a good 2.5 cm/1 inch gap at the top. Seal the jar and leave in a warm place for 2 days to ferment. Chill before serving in glasses with slices of lemon.

STRAWBERRY SODA

This vibrant, healthy fizzy drink also works well with other fruits. If you use raspberries, it is best to strain them before you add the water kefir.

Makes about 1.1 litres/ 2 pints/ 4²/₃ cups

400 g/14 oz/2¾ cups ripe sweet strawberries
750 ml/1¼ pints/3¼ cups water kefir (*see* page 114)
unrefined cane sugar, to taste (optional)

Blitz the strawberries in a blender until completely smooth. Taste and if they are sour add a spoonful of sugar. Add the kefir and blend again.

Pour the strawberry soda into flip-top bottles and seal tightly. Leave in a warm place out of direct sunlight for 12–24 hours. Check the bottles occasionally, making sure they do not build up too much pressure. If necessary, open to release some of the gas.

When the soda is ready, chill before serving.

Serving suggestion: place some ice cubes and sliced strawberries in a tall glass, pour over the strawberry soda, fix a whole strawberry and lemon wedge on the side of the glass and serve.

GINGER BEER

The ginger beer produced using a ginger beer plant has a subtle flavour unlike anything bought in the shops. If you don't have time to make your own ginger beer plant, you can find them online.

Makes 2.25 litres/4 pints/9½ cups

250 g/9 oz/1¼ cups unrefined cane sugar
2 litres/3½ pints/8½ cups water
strained liquid from ginger beer plant (*see* overleaf)
juice of 1 lemon
25 ml/1 fl oz/2 tbsp ginger juice – if you do not have a juicer, grate a medium size piece of ginger and tie up in a muslin (cheesecloth) bag

Place the sugar and water into a large jug or bowl and stir well to dissolve the sugar. Add the strained liquid from the ginger beer plant, the lemon juice and ginger juice, or the ginger tied up in a muslin (cheesecloth) bag and mix well.

Seal with a lid or cover with a cloth and leave for about 5 days (or until it tastes just a little sweeter than you would like the finished product to be), then using a funnel, carefully pour into your chosen bottles.

Leave in a cool place and it should be ready to drink within 2–3 days. If you are using glass bottles, check regularly to ensure the gas does not reach explosive levels. Once you are happy with the level of fizz, store in the refrigerator for up to 3 days before drinking.

GINGER BEER PLANT

Place 1 tablespoon fresh ginger cut into small cubes into a 1 litre/1¾ pint/34 oz glass jar three-quarters full of filtered water. Stir in 2 teaspoons sugar.

Cover the top of the jar with muslin (cheesecloth) and leave on the side in the kitchen. Every day for the next 7 days, add 2 teaspoons sugar and 2 teaspoons fresh diced ginger and stir well.

After a week, the mixture should be bubbling and ready to use. If not, carry on feeding for a little longer.

When the plant is ready, cover a strainer with muslin (cheesecloth) and strain the mix into a bowl. Keep the solid matter for your next plant and use the liquid as the base for ginger beer.

FRUIT SHRUB

A shrub is a fruit and vinegar syrup. To ensure its health benefits you must use a raw apple cider vinegar. Mixed with fizzy water, it makes a refreshing, tart and tangy drink. A splash of shrub lifts a yogurt and fruit smoothie. You can use lots of different fruits to make a shrub, but the soft berries like redcurrants, raspberries and blackberries work best.

soft berries
unrefined cane sugar
raw apple cider vinegar

Gently mash the berries in a bowl and mix with sugar. For every 500 g/1 lb 2 oz fruit add 250 g/9 oz /1¼ cups sugar. Cover the bowl and leave to stand in the kitchen for 2 days, stirring once a day.

After 2 days, strain the mixture, pushing through as much as you can. Measure the syrup, then combine equal amounts of syrup and raw apple cider vinegar together. Pour into flip-top, screw or cork-topped bottles. Store in the refrigerator or a cool, dark place and consume within 6 months.

HONEY HERBAL ELIXIR

Honey and herbs together enhance each other's medicinal properties.
Lightly fermented honey drinks are some of the oldest known beverages.
Serve as a restorative tonic.

Makes about 2.5 litres/ 4¹/₂ pints/ 10¹/₂ cups

large bunch chamomile, sage, thyme, rosemary, lemon balm,
    elderflower or fennel; combinations work, as does adding spices
    like ginger, cinnamon and star anise
2.25 litres/4 pints/9½ cups filtered water
350 g/12 oz/1 cup raw honey

Put your chosen herb or combination of herbs and spices in a heatproof bowl.
Bring the water to the boil and pour over the herbs. Cover with a dish towel and
leave to infuse for 24 hours. Strain into a large glass jar, add the honey and stir
until dissolved. Seal with a lid or cover with muslin (cheesecloth) and leave in a
warm place for 3 days.

Pour into flip-top bottles and seal tightly. Place in a cool, dry place, checking
occasionally to ensure the bottles do not build up pressure. Consume within
2 months.

KOMBUCHA

Probiotic kombucha tea has been used for generations to help strengthen the immune system.

Makes about 2 litres/ 3¹/₂ pints/ 8¹/₂ cups

4 black tea bags
175 g/6 oz/scant 1 cup unrefined cane sugar
200 ml/7 fl oz/¾ cup kombucha from a previous batch, if this is not available use 2 tbsp raw apple cider vinegar (*see* page 116)
1 kombucha 'mother'

Make a pot of tea using the tea bags and leave to brew for 30 minutes.

Strain the tea into a measuring jug or cup, add the sugar and stir until it dissolves, then make up to 2 litres/3½ pints/8½ cups with cold filtered water.

Stir in the kombucha from the previous batch or the vinegar. Pour into a wide-mouthed glass jar or bowl and add the kombucha 'mother'. Cover with muslin (cheesecloth) or a dish towel and fasten securely with a rubber band.

Leave to ferment in a warm, dark place for around 10 days, checking regularly. You may notice a film developing on the surface – this is a new kombucha 'mother'.

Pour the kombucha into a flip-top bottle, reserving some for the next batch. Store in the refrigerator and consume within a week. The 'mother' or SCOBY needs regular nourishment, so once you start making kombucha it's good to maintain a rhythm.

AVOCADO SMOOTHIE

This is a very nourishing, creamy avocado smoothie. You can also make this smoothie with coconut kefir, if liked.

Serves 2

1 avocado

500 ml/18 fl oz/2 cups almond milk kefir (*see* page 112)

1 large handful spinach

splash ume plum seasoning

pinch chilli powder

salt and freshly ground black pepper

To garnish:

parsley leaves

1 tomato, seeded and diced

Halve, pit and scoop out the avocado flesh into a blender. Add all the remaining ingredients, except the tomato and parsley, and blend until smooth. Pour into glasses, add a flourish of parsley leaves and tomato and enjoy!

SOUPS

MISO SOUP

Miso soup and rice, with a side dish of pickles and a cup of tea is a traditional meal in Japan.

Serves 4

750 ml/1¼ pints/3¼ cups dashi (*see* page 102)

8 fresh shiitake mushrooms, thinly sliced

225 g/8 oz kale or mustard greens, chopped

1 chilli, finely chopped

1 handful flat-leaf parsley, chopped

8 tsp red rice miso paste

1 tsp mirin

2 tbsp water

Additional options:

small cubes tofu

spring onions (scallions), finely sliced

shredded nori seaweed

fine ginger slivers

Bring the dashi to the boil in a pan. Add the shiitake, kale or mustard greens, chilli and parsley, reduce the heat and simmer for 10 minutes.

Remove from the heat and leave to stand for 3 minutes.

Mix the miso, mirin and water together in a small bowl and add to the soup, along with any additional options. Stir well and serve.

BROCCOLI MISO SOUP

Add the miso after you have removed the soup from the heat to preserve
the beneficial microorganisms and enzymes.

Serves 4

2 tbsp olive oil

2 garlic cloves, peeled and finely chopped

1 green chilli, seeded and finely chopped

500 g/1 lb 2oz/7 cups broccoli florets

2 tsp chopped thyme

750 ml/1¼ pints/3¼ cups dashi (*see* page 102)

8 oyster mushrooms

1 tsp lime juice

4 tsp red miso paste

2 tsp shoyu soy sauce

2 tbsp water

freshly ground black pepper

Heat 1 tbsp olive oil in a pan and gently cook the garlic and chilli
for 2 minutes. Add the broccoli, thyme and dashi, bring to the boil,
then reduce the heat and simmer for 5 minutes. Remove from the
heat, cool slightly, then blitz in a blender until smooth. Return to
the pan.

Heat the remaining olive oil in a frying pan and cook the
mushrooms for 2 minutes on each side, then reserve.

Mix the lime juice, miso, soy sauce and water together.

Bring the soup to the boil, then remove from the heat. Whisk in the miso mixture, taste and adjust seasoning as necessary. Serve in bowls, topping each one with 2 mushrooms and a twist of black pepper.

BEETROOT SOUP WITH KEFIR

This is a delicious cold beetroot soup that maintains all the benefits of kefir.

Serves 4

700 g/1½ lb/scant 5¼ cups beetroot (beets), peeled and diced

2 red onions, peeled and diced

1 tbsp olive oil

2 tsp chopped dill

750 ml/1¼ pints/3¼ cups kefir (*see* page 110)

salt and freshly ground black pepper

To garnish:

4 finely sliced radishes

handful mint leaves

8 walnuts

Preheat the oven to 220°C/425°F/Gas Mark 7.

Toss the beetroot (beets) and onions in the olive oil and roast them in the oven until just beginning to caramelize. Leave to cool.

Blend the dill, kefir, beetroot and onions in a blender until smooth.
Taste and season as necessary with salt and freshly ground black pepper.

Serve in bowls, topped with radishes, mint, walnuts or whatever you choose.

SAUERKRAUT SOUP WITH BEETROOT, POTATOES & PEARL BARLEY

Serves 4–6

150 g/5 oz/scant ¾ cup pearl barley

1 tbsp olive oil

4 shallots, peeled and finely sliced

3 garlic cloves, peeled and finely diced

3 medium beetroot (beets), peeled and diced

2 medium potatoes, scrubbed and diced

1 litre/1¾ pints/4 cups dashi (*see* page 102)

2 tbsp flat-leaf parsley, chopped

1 tbsp thyme, finely chopped

freshly ground black pepper

6 tbsp sauerkraut (*see* page 96)

1 tbsp flat-leaf parsley leaves

Place the pearl barley in a pan, cover with water and cook for 30 minutes, then strain and set aside.

Heat the oil in a medium pan and gently cook the shallots and garlic for 2 minutes. Add the beetroot (beets) and potatoes and cook for a further 5 minutes. Add the dashi to the pan together with the herbs. Bring to the boil, reduce the heat and simmer for 30 minutes, or until the vegetables are tender.

Add the cooked barley and cook for a further 5 minutes. Season well with black pepper. Remove from the heat, stir in the sauerkraut and serve with a few flat-leaf parsley leaves on top.

MAIN DISHES

TEMPEH STIR-FRY WITH GREEN VEG

When broccoli and courgette are not in season you can substitute with other green vegetables. Pak choi and green beans work really well.

Serves 4

200 g/7 oz tempeh (*see* page 100), cut into small cubes

2 tbsp coconut oil

2 onions, peeled and finely sliced

350 g/12 oz broccoli, cut into small florets

175 g/6 oz courgette (zucchini), cut into rounds

150 ml/¼ pint/⅔ cup coconut milk

For the marinade:

juice and zest of 1 lime

2 tbsp tamari

1 tbsp sesame oil; 1 teaspoon mirin

thumb ginger, peeled and grated

3 garlic cloves, peeled and very finely chopped

Combine all the marinade ingredients together in a bowl and mix well. Toss in the tempeh and leave to marinate for 2 hours at room temperature. Meanwhile, heat 1 tablespoon coconut oil in a wok, add the onions and stir-fry for 2 minutes until soft. Add the broccoli and courgette (zucchini) and stir-fry for 2–3 minutes, then transfer to a bowl.

Remove the tempeh from the marinade. Heat the remaining coconut oil in the wok, add the tempeh and stir-fry until lightly golden. Transfer to a bowl and keep warm. Wipe out the wok and add the marinade and coconut milk, mixing well. Toss in the broccoli mixture and heat through. Serve, topped with the tempeh.

SALMON WITH TOMATOES & CAPERS ON SAUERKRAUT

The essential fatty acids in wild salmon and the beneficial bacteria in sauerkraut make this a particularly nourishing dish.

Serves 4

4 wild salmon fillets

salt and freshly ground black pepper

olive oil, for oiling and brushing

2 tsp butter

4 shallots, peeled and finely sliced

6 tomatoes, quartered, seeded and diced

2 tbsp capers

1 tbsp crème fraîche

6 tbsp sauerkraut (*see* page 96)

Preheat the grill to a hot setting.

Season the salmon liberally with salt and pepper, then place them in a lightly oiled baking dish and brush with oil. Grill without turning for about 8 minutes taking care not to overcook.

Meanwhile, gently heat the butter in a pan, add the shallots and fry for 1 minute. Add the tomatoes, capers and crème fraîche, mix well and keep warm.

Arrange the sauerkraut in a serving dish and place the salmon on top. Spoon over the tomato and caper mixture and serve.

SQUASH STUFFED WITH TEMPEH

This recipe works very well with pea tempeh, but if you are unable to make your own pea tempeh, substitute it with bought soy tempeh.

Serves 4

4 squash, 1 for each person (acorn squash, sweet dumpling or summer patty pan)

2 tbsp olive oil, plus extra for oiling

4 shallots, peeled and finely sliced

4 garlic cloves, peeled and finely chopped

175 g/6 oz/1¾ cups button mushrooms

175 g/6 oz/generous 1 cup cherry tomatoes

225 g/8 oz pea tempeh (*see* page 100)

handful mint leaves, roughly torn

salt and freshly ground black pepper

Preheat the oven to 190°C/375°F/Gas Mark 5.

Cut a lid off the top of the squash and reserve. Scoop the seeds out of the squash.

Place the squash, cut-side down, in a very lightly oiled ovenproof dish, pour in 5mm/¼ inch water and bake in the oven for 20 minutes. Carefully turn the squash the right way up and pop on the reserved squash lids. Return to the oven and cook for a further 10 minutes. When the squash is soft, but not too soft, remove from the oven. The exact cooking time will depend on the size and variety of the squash.

Meanwhile, prepare the filling. Heat the oil in a pan and cook the shallots and garlic until soft. Add the mushrooms and cook for a further 4–5 minutes until the mixture is just beginning to caramelize. Toss in the tomatoes and when they begin to break down, crumble in the tempeh and cook for 2 minutes. Add the mint and season well.

Remove the squash lids and fill the cavities with the tempeh mixture, pop the lids back on and serve.

TEMPEH SANDWICH

A substantial sandwich for when you are feeling more than peckish.

Serves 1

1 tsp shoyu soy sauce

1 tsp olive oil

3 slices tempeh (*see* page 100)

2 tsp almond butter

2 slices sourdough bread

1 tsp red miso paste

handful alfalfa sprouts

few red onion rings

4 slices cucumber

1 tomato, cut into slices

2 lettuce leaves

Mix the shoyu and oil together and brush onto the tempeh slices. Heat a pan and cook the tempeh on both sides until crisp.

Spread the almond butter over one side of each of the slices of bread, then spread the miso on top.

Pile the tempeh and the remaining ingredients between the slices of bread and serve.

GRAINS, BREADS
& TREATS

FERMENTED WHOLE OAT PORRIDGE

By fermenting the whole oat groats before cooking, the flavour of porridge is greatly enhanced and the grains are far more digestible. Typical of many ferments, fermented whole oat porridge is more about the method than exact quantities. A groat is a whole oat with the husk removed.

Place the required amount of oat groats in a bowl, cover with filtered water and loosely cover with muslin (cheesecloth). Leave at room temperature for 2 days. To speed up the process, add 1 tablespoon sauerkraut juice, raw apple cider vinegar or milk kefir to the water.

Depending on your flavour preference, you can either cook the oats in their soaking liquid or strain and cook in fresh water. Pop the oats in a pan, cover with your chosen liquid, bring gently to a simmer and cook over a low heat, very slowly, until thick and creamy. Add a pinch of salt and serve with fruit or whatever you fancy. You can also eat the oats as they are without cooking.

SOURDOUGH RYE BREAD

This simple rye bread is about texture, consistency and trusting your intuition. Here is a basic method. Make sure your leaven is active by feeding it well the night before you use it.

Makes 2 small loaves

oil, for oiling

coriander or caraway seeds, for sprinkling

250 g/9 oz rye leaven (*see* page 92)

500 g/1 lb 2 oz/5 cups rye flour, plus extra for sprinkling

1 tsp salt

2 tsp molasses (optional)

Oil two loaf tins, about 16 x 11 cm/6¼ x 4¼ inches, and sprinkle coriander or caraway seeds on the base.

Mix the leaven, flour, salt and molasses (if using) in a bowl, adding enough water to form a soft, sticky dough. Halve the dough and, using wet hands, shape each half into a loaf shape and pop them into the prepared tins. Flatten the dough in each tin with a spatula and sprinkle a little flour over each one. Cover and leave in a warm place for 5 hours, or until doubled in size.

Preheat the oven to 220°C/425°F/Gas Mark 7, 20 minutes before baking.

Bake for about 45 minutes. Check after 30 minutes and if the loaf is becoming too brown, reduce the temperature to 190°C/ 375°F/ Gas Mark 5 for the last 15 minutes. Turn out and cool on a wire rack.

BUCKWHEAT PANCAKES

These gluten-free fermented pancakes are simple to make and easy to digest. Serve the pancakes with anything you fancy, savoury or sweet. Any unused batter can be kept in the refrigerator for 3 days.

Makes about 6 pancakes

275 g/10 oz/generous 1⅓ cups buckwheat groats
2 tbsp sauerkraut juice or kefir (*see* pages 96 and 110)
1 tsp salt
ghee or coconut oil

Place the buckwheat in a bowl, pour in enough water to cover and soak overnight.

Next day, drain the buckwheat and rinse well, then put in a blender and blend with the sauerkraut juice or kefir, salt and enough water so that it reaches the consistency of smooth pancake batter. Pour into a large jug (pitcher), cover and leave in a warm place for 12–18 hours.

Heat a frying pan and swirl a little ghee or coconut oil around the base, then pour in enough batter to cover the pan and make a pancake that is not too thick. Cook all the way through before flipping over and cooking for a further minute, then sliding out onto a plate. Repeat.

SAMBAR IDLI

Idli are a classic Southern Indian dish. They are most often eaten at breakfast or as a snack. They are steamed patties made from a fermented rice and dhal batter and usually served with chutney, dry spice dip or sambar.

Makes about 20–24 idlis/ serves 4

For the sambar:

150 g/5 oz/¾ cup dhal (split peas, lentils or mung beans)

3 tomatoes, roughly chopped

2 carrots, scrubbed and sliced

2 red onions, peeled and diced

1 tsp sambar powder

½ tsp ground turmeric

about 300 ml/½ pint/1¼ cups water

1 tbsp tamarind pulp

1 tsp sesame oil

1 tsp mustard seeds

2 garlic cloves, peeled and finely chopped

¼ tsp asafoetida

¼ tsp fenugreek seeds

¼ tsp chilli powder

handful coriander (cilantro), roughly chopped

For the idlis:

a little oil, for oiling

1 quantity idli, dosa and uttapam batter (*see* page 94)

To make the sambar, soak the dhal for 1 hour. Drain and put into a pan with the tomatoes, carrots, onions, sambar powder and turmeric. Pour in the water or enough to cover and bring to the boil. Reduce the heat, cover and simmer gently until the dhal is well cooked and mushy. Remove from the heat and stir in the tamarind pulp.

Heat the sesame oil in a small pan, add the mustard seeds and when they begin to crackle, add the garlic and cook gently for 1 minute. Add the asafoetida, fenugreek and chilli, stir well and remove from the heat. Add this spice mixture along with the coriander (cilantro) to the dhal, then pour the sambar into a serving dish to accompany the idlis.

To cook the idlis, lightly oil your idli moulds and carefully pour in the batter, which should be a thick pouring consistency. Set the mould tier over boiling water, cover and steam over a medium heat for 10 minutes, or until firm.

Loosen the idlis and remove from the moulds, pile onto a plate and repeat with more batter until you have the number you require. Store any remaining batter in the refrigerator. Serve with sambar.

AVAL DOSA

A thin Southern Indian fried pancake typically served with chutney.
The flavour should be sour, so it is best made with a 2–3 day-old batter.

Makes about 12–16 dosas

1 quantity idli, dosa and uttapam batter (*see* page 94)
1 tsp fenugreek seeds
coconut oil, for cooking
tomato or coconut chutney, to serve

Add enough water to the batter to make a good pouring consistency, then stir in the fenugreek seeds.

Heat a frying pan and swirl a little coconut oil around the base, then pour in enough batter that when you gently swirl the pan, it makes a thin pancake. Do not make the pancake too thin, as the soft batter may tear. The dosa will develop tiny holes over the surface. Put a little oil around the edges of the pancake, cover and steam cook for 1 minute, or until firm and just colouring at the edges. Do not flip, but lift the dosa from the pan and slide onto a plate.

Serve hot with chutney.

UTTAPAM

A thick fermented pancake to which vegetables, traditionally tomatoes and onions, and chillies, are added.

Makes 8–10 uttapams

1 quantity idli, dosa and uttapam batter (*see* page 94)
1 tsp ground fennel seeds
ghee or coconut oil, for cooking
2 medium red onions, peeled and finely sliced
4 tomatoes, seeded and finely diced
2 green chillies, finely diced
handful coriander (cilantro), chopped
chutney, to serve (optional)

Add water as necessary to the batter to make a good pouring consistency, then stir in the ground fennel seeds.

Heat a frying pan and swirl a little ghee or coconut oil around the base. Ladle the batter into the pan, then using the back of the ladle, spread the batter out in a circular motion to form a thick pancake. Let the bottom set, then while the top is still liquid, top with the onions, tomatoes, chillies and coriander (cilantro). Dot some ghee or oil around the edges and on top and cook for 2 minutes, or until the top is set. Flip over and cook on the other side until the vegetables are slightly charred.

Serve as they are or with chutney.

INJERA

A staple of Ethiopian meals, injera is a large, flat, spongy bread made from teff, a grain indigenous to Ethiopia

Makes 4–6

200 g/7 oz/2 cups teff flour
450 ml/¾ pint/1¾ cups water
½ tsp salt
ghee or sesame oil

Place the flour and water in a bowl and beat well together. Cover and leave in a warm place for 24 hours.

When you are ready to use the batter, stir in the salt. Heat a frying pan and swirl a little ghee or sesame oil around the base. Pour enough batter into the pan to entirely cover the surface, reduce the heat and cover with a lid to retain the moisture. It will take about 7–8 minutes to cook through. When the bubbles on top dry out, the injera is ready.

Slide the injera out of the pan onto a plate and repeat. Place parchment paper between each injera as you stack them to prevent them sticking together. Any leftover batter can be stored in the refrigerator.

CHIA KEFIR PUDDING

Chia seeds are native to South America. Aztec warriors would eat chia seeds to give them high energy and endurance.

Makes 4 small puddings

300 ml/½ pint/1¼ cups kefir (*see* page 110)
4 tbsp chia seeds
dried strawberries and hazelnuts, to serve

Mix the kefir and chia seeds together in a bowl and rest for 3 minutes. Stir well and rest again for 3 minutes. Divide between four small dishes and chill for 2–3 hours, or overnight.

To serve, top the puddings with a few dried strawberries and hazelnuts.

VARIATIONS Flavour with a little vanilla, lemon zest or ground cinnamon and sweeten with a swirl of maple syrup, orange juice or fresh fruit purée.

CHOCOLATE KEFIR PUDDING

Kefir cheese is rich in probiotic microorganisms. Blend with egg yolks, honey and chocolate for a really luscious dessert.

Serves 4

3 egg yolks

2 tbsp raw (unpasteurized, unprocessed) honey

200 g/7 oz bitter chocolate, broken into pieces

100 ml/3½ fl oz/⅓ cup almond milk

225 g/8 oz/1 cup kefir cheese (*see* below)

For the kefir cheese:

600 ml/1 pint/2½ cups dairy milk kefir (*see* page 110)

To decorate:

crème fraîche

mint leaves

raw cacao powder

To make the kefir cheese, drape a piece of muslin (cheesecloth) over a strainer set over a bowl. Pour the kefir into the strainer, gather up the sides to cover and chill overnight.

Next day, the kefir cheese is in the strainer and kefir whey in the bowl. You will need 225 g/8 oz/1 cup kefir cheese for this recipe.

For the pudding, whisk the egg yolks and honey together in another bowl until very thick and light.

Gently melt the chocolate in a heatproof bowl set over a pan of barely simmering water.

Blend the almond milk, kefir cheese, egg mixture and melted chocolate in a blender until smooth. Divide between four dishes and chill for 1 hour.

To serve, top each dish with a dollop of crème fraîche and a few mint leaves and a scattering of cacao powder

YOGURT ICE CREAM

To make a soft, smooth and creamy frozen yogurt, you need to add add
sugar or honey, as this prevents large hard crystals forming. You need
to make this frozen dessert from a reasonably thick yogurt. If yours is
on the runny side use 1.7 litres/3 pints/6 cups and strain through muslin
(cheesecloth) for 30 minutes.

Serves 6

1.1 litres/2 pints/4⅔ cups full-fat plain live yogurt
175 g/6 oz/½ cup raw (unpasteurized, unprocessed) acacia honey
good pinch salt
1 tsp vanilla extract

Whisk all the ingredients together in a stainless-steel bowl. Chill for 1 hour,
then whisk well again and freeze for a further 1 hour.

Remove the mixture, beat well to break up the frozen parts and return to the
freezer. Repeat twice more at 30-minute intervals, then transfer to a covered
storage container until ready to use.

Alternatively, you can freeze the mixture in an ice-cream machine according
to the manufacturer's instructions.

INDEX

Entries with upper-case initials
indicate recipes.

If you enjoyed this book please sign up for updates,
information and offers on further titles in this series at
www.flametreepublishing.com